THE DIRECTOR
AS COLLABORATOR

THE DIRECTOR AS COLLABORATOR

ROBERT KNOPF

University at Buffalo

PEARSON

Boston ■ New York ■ San Francisco ■ Mexico City ■ Montreal
Toronto ■ London ■ Madrid ■ Munich ■ Paris ■ Hong Kong
Singapore ■ Tokyo ■ Cape Town ■ Sydney

Series Editor: *Molly Taylor*
Series Editorial Assistant: *Suzanne Stradley*
Marketing Manager: *Mandee Eckersley*
Senior Production Editor: *Beth Houston*
Editorial Production Service: *Walsh & Associates, Inc.*
Composition Buyer: *Linda Cox*
Manufacturing Buyer: *JoAnne Sweeney*
Electronic Composition: *Publishers' Design and Production Services, Inc.*
Cover Administrator: *Kristina Mose-Libon*

For related titles and support materials, visit our online catalog at www.ablongman.com.

Between the time website information is gathered and then published, it is not unusual for some sites to have closed. Also, the transcription of URLs can result in typographical errors. The publisher would appreciate notification where these errors occur so that they may be corrected in subsequent editions.

Library of Congress Cataloging-in-Publication Data

Knopf, Robert
      The director as collaborator / Robert Knopf. — 1st ed.
         p. cm.
      Includes bibliographical references and index.
      ISBN 0-205-39709-3
         1. Theater—Production and direction.   I. Title.

   PN2053.K58 2006
   792.02'33'092—dc22   2005050936

Printed in the United States of America

10 9 8 7 6 5 4 3 2 1   09 08 07 06 05

To Liz, Ally, and Lara, my favorite collaborators

CONTENTS

Acknowledgments   xi

Introduction   1

What Is Collaboration?   2

The Core Action   6

The Responsibilities of Collaboration   8

Fundamental Techniques   9

Supplemental Reading   13

1   Collaboration and Leadership   15

Balancing Leadership and Collaboration   16

Supplemental Reading   20

2   Core Action   21

Story and Plot   21

Exercise Critique   25

Action Analysis   27

Script Analysis   28

Key Terms   32

Supplemental Reading   33

3   Collaboration in Rehearsal   35

The First Scene Collaboration   38

Preparation   42

Sample Rehearsal Schedule   44

Rehearsal Observations   44

Videotaping Rehearsals   46

Supplemental Reading   46

4   Directing Elements   47

Textual Elements   49
Structure   49
Actions and Objectives   55
Shifts and Key Moments   59
Groundplan   62
Character   68
Relationship and Status   71
Language   75

Visceral Elements   76
Tempo and Rhythm   77
Sound and Mood   79
Visual Composition   82
Movement   87
Gesture   91
Environment   92
Style   94

Integrating Directing Elements   96

Script Analysis   98

Dramaturgy Checklist   99

5   Design Collaboration   101

Core Action Statements   104
Hedda Gabler by Henrik Ibsen   106
The Baltimore Waltz by Paula Vogel   109
The Birthday Party by Harold Pinter   111
Twelfth Night by William Shakespeare   113

Design Timetable   117

Key Terms   124

Supplemental Reading   127

6   Other Collaborators   129

Playwrights   129
Readings and Staged Readings   129

Dramaturgs   131

Music Directors and Choreographers   132

Key Terms   133

7   Auditions and Casting   135

Casting the One-Act Plays   137

Audition Goals   138

Supplemental Reading   139

APPENDIX A   Forms   141
    Project Proposal Form   142
    Sample Audition Notice   143
    Audition Form   144
    Sample Callback Form   145
    Sample Cast List   146
    Rehearsal Observation Form   147
    Producing Checklist   148
    Program Information   149
    Poster Information   150
    Course Outline   151

APPENDIX B   Glossary of Key Terms   153

APPENDIX C   Bibliography of One-Act Plays   159

APPENDIX D   Selected Bibliography   163
    Directing   163
    Acting   165
    Design   166
    Playwriting   168
    Dramaturgy   168
    Ensembles   168
    Theater History and Theory   168
    Management   171
    Publicity   171

Index   173

ACKNOWLEDGMENTS

I would like to thank several people who were instrumental in the development of this book. My editors at Allyn and Bacon, Molly Taylor and Michael Kish, helped me make decisions about revisions and keep the focus of the book on developing directors. Jeremy Make was a tireless research assistant, working on the preliminary versions of the bibliographies and taking time to switch to whatever task was needed at the time. I can only hope that my directing students over the years have learned as much from me as I have from them. The following reviewers provided invaluable feedback on the structure and content of the book: Christopher Berchild, Indiana State University; Marnie Brennan, Harrisburg Area Community College; Terry Converse, Washington State University; Rebecca Daniels, St. Lawrence University; Phoebe Hall, Fayetteville State University; Luigi Salerni, University of Illinois-Chicago; and Arno Selco, Ithaca College. I value their insights into directing pedagogy greatly; they helped me refine the overall vision of the book in countless ways. Mike Gauger suggested numerous ways to streamline the first three chapters and find the voice of this book.

I would also like to thank those theater artists with whom I have worked most closely for their influence on my development as a director and teacher: Erica Gould, Erik Jensen, Lawrence Klavan, Vince Mountain, Danielle Quisenberry, Matt Richards, Dara Seitzman, and Danny Zorn. Last, I am always thankful for the support of my family. My parents taught an only child how to collaborate (a feat worthy of a book in and of itself). My wife, Liz, and daughters, Ally and Lara, were exceptionally patient as I labored to complete this book. I am indebted to them for always believing in me, and they will always be my most beloved collaborators.

Introduction

Titles possess great significance for most directors. The title of this book, *The Director as Collaborator*, might strike you as intriguing or as a contradiction in terms, depending upon your experience with directors and as a director. If you think of the director as the dominant force in creating the production, the idea of collaborating with an ensemble of actors, designers, technical staff, and, in some cases, a dramaturg or playwright, might at first seem to require directors to give up too much artistic control. Some of you might believe that directing is collaborative by nature, and that the title of this book is redundant. But most directors combine aspects of collaboration with more "controlling" working methods, falling between what we might call the purely authoritarian and the purely collaborative. Theater can offer the director tremendous opportunities for collaboration, yet not every director takes full advantage of these opportunities, even though directors and productions benefit enormously from keeping collaboration integral to the process.

Directors collaborate in many ways, depending upon their personalities, styles, experiences, the play, the venue, the ensemble, the production company, and the rehearsal schedule. This book does not require you to adhere to a strict method or system of collaboration, but it is designed to encourage you to experiment with collaborative methods of directing and discover how collaboration works for you, to help you add collaboration to the tools in your director's "toolbox" so that you can use it when and as you see fit. The purpose is not to force you to collaborate all the time—such an approach is neither practical nor desirable—but to expand the range of collaborative tools at your disposal and encourage you to look for productive opportunities for collaboration, ones that will improve your directing process and product. Collaboration does not preclude leadership; rather, it is a style of leadership.

Throughout this book, I will be asking you to collaborate with one another on group exercises and to direct short scenes and plays; to complete most of the exercises, you will have to collaborate to learn directing skills. The structure of the exercises also encourages you to experiment with different solutions to the challenges of a variety of fundamental directing problems and skills, from script analysis and working with your ensemble to physical, aural, and visual elements of staging. You will undertake these theatrical experiments *before* discussing the principles at work in detail. After each set of exercises, you will find discussion questions and a set of defined terms. Read the terms provided at the end of each chapter only after you try the exercises. Learn by experiencing, then solidify your knowledge and acquire the terminology that professionals use to describe what you've learned. Don't be afraid to try something new, even if you ultimately discover that it doesn't work; as the slogan of the O'Neill National Theatre Institute puts it, "Risk. Fail. Risk again." Experiment and risk are essential elements of creativity and collaboration; asking good questions and trying out possible solutions are perhaps more important than learning the established wisdom.

Almost all productions benefit from the director's collaborative spirit, although the rehearsal circumstances might suggest how and to what extent you collaborate as a director. In the creative process, constructive collaboration helps bring more ideas into the process and encourage each member of the ensemble to see his or her contributions as significant, "to own the production." When the ensemble members feel as though they own their contributions to a production, the collaboration and process generate energy, commitment, and creativity in the total ensemble. Encouraging everyone in the ensemble to create a part of the production rather than simply to execute the director's detailed ideas not only engenders goodwill, but it also gets each person's mind working toward the same end and frequently breaks down the traditional barriers and more-than-occasional rifts between production areas. In this way, collaborative directing can improve the work environment of the ensemble, and a better environment helps stimulate better work.

What Is Collaboration?

There are no absolute truisms about collaboration, but some general principles might be useful for you to begin to acquire collaborative skills. Under most circumstances, collaboration assumes that no one person has all the best ideas about the production. Instead, collaboration presumes that the combination of talents and ideas of the ensemble will be greater than the sum of its parts, and certainly greater than any one part (i.e., the director's). If collaboration becomes a part of your directing method, it will affect your directing priorities. You might, for example, choose to work with actors, designers, and staff who share an interest in collaboration—many young theater companies have been formed on the basis of this shared interest—and are looking for this kind of theater experience. In these situations, the person who seems initially to be the most talented or experienced for the job might not always be the best choice for your ensemble. The desire to collaborate is imperative; absent that desire, you might be unable to create an environment within which collaboration thrives.

The director began as an authoritarian figure. The first director, if we regard directing history from the advent of the title "director" in the nineteenth century, is widely believed to be Georg II, the duke of Saxe-Meiningen; directing his servants in large scenes with nearly unlimited rehearsal time, he had about as much artistic authority as any director could imagine. Although some scholars regard his stage manager, Ludwig Chronegk, as the first director—and indeed the duke eventually named him the stage director for the Meiningen Players—for our purposes the significance of the Meiningen Players is that the director, be it the duke or Chronegk, wielded tremendous power because of the duke's position as a member of the nobility. For a variety of reasons, most directors still use authoritarian models of directing. The history of the theater director as primary creator—sometimes usurping the playwright's artistic contribution—has produced many generations of more authoritarian directors. Stanislavski's earliest directing notebooks illustrate how he would prepare to direct a production by marking down even the most minute details of each character's physical actions. Although ensembles have challenged this model along the way, from the Living Theater to the Mabou Mines to Theatre de Complicité, one or two central artists (generally directors) usually guided these more "utopian" enterprises. The mainstream of directing practice, under the economic pressure to produce profitable (or at least not tremendously unprofitable) productions, has tended to conform to this more authoritarian model of the director because it tends to be quicker and easier, and puts the responsibility for the final product on a single person: the director. But this need not be the case. You can learn more by sharing responsibility, by balancing collaboration and leadership, and by working toward an ensemble.

We reach collaboration and consensus only through trust and belief in our partners. Creation of trust requires time for an ensemble to develop a shared language and vision and to learn to treat each other's ideas with respect, even if some ideas will inevitably be rejected. To do this, the director should allow constructive failure and encourage risk taking. Under some circumstances—such as an extremely truncated rehearsal period with an ensemble that has never worked together before—the time available for collaboration might be limited. For the director, it's best to shape the process to the circumstances of the individual production. Make the process clear to the ensemble at the start of the rehearsal period, so that its members know what they might expect and what you expect of them.

The creation of trust in the creative process starts with a clear understanding of each person's responsibilities. Most issues that arise from a lack of trust in rehearsal and design stem from misunderstandings about what each person does, a situation that creates "turf battles." In other words, if the ensemble members do not know the boundaries between their work and that of their collaborators, it is difficult for the director to create a trusting environment, since contributions to the creative endeavor can be seen as crossing these oft-times hidden or disputed boundaries.

An Actor Collaborates

Collaboration comes from trust. If a director asks me to do something, I don't care how outlandish or daring it seems, I do it. I don't second-guess. If something doesn't work then it won't fly. No director wants to look like an idiot, so I have faith that if it truly is a howler he won't let it stay. He'll just say, "Brave choice, wrong play."

Some of the most fun I have ever had in rehearsals came from seemingly idiotic ideas that led the ensemble to a fantastic new place that we never would have found without wading through a load of sludge. When I was doing *Ivanov*, the director, Gerry Gutierrez, told me that I should laugh after every line in a different way. *Every* line mind you. So I laughed. I tittered. I guffawed. I snorted. I cackled. I eventually wept because I was so mortified: my first Broadway play and I was being such a dork!

Well, I became so irritating that the cast, which included Kevin Kline, started to wince every time I spoke because they couldn't imagine what shriek was going to come out of me next. It was perfect. The character, Marfusha Babakina, was a bumbling idiot who no one really liked. So throughout the first week of rehearsals everyone came to either wince, cringe, giggle, or shake their heads every time I opened my mouth. I managed to keep my sense of humor about it and completely committed to it.

The next week Gerry told me I could pick three places to laugh . . . but never the same three. By the time we opened I was down to one laugh a night and not one actor could take their eyes off me on the stage. It had turned into this great tension-filled game, because often other actors would laugh with me, and here was the director's stroke of genius: no one was supposed to find me the slightest bit amusing. Now if someone had told me that was going to be the end result, I never would have believed them. But it was just electric on stage.

Directors have ideas. They are good ideas, but they are ideas waiting for the actor to commit to them, and make them better.

—Judith Hawking, actress

Judith Hawking has appeared on Broadway in *Ivanov* and *Voices in the Dark*. She has acted Off-Broadway at the Public Theater, the Signature Theatre, and Playwrights Horizons, and regionally at American Repertory Theatre, McCarter Theatre, Arena Stage, Long Wharf Theatre, and Cleveland Playhouse, among many others.

Within most theatrical endeavors, the director's responsibilities include leadership, a role that can be fulfilled in many ways. Leadership does not preclude collaboration; in theater, these concepts can be complementary. Collaborative directors can support and challenge their ensemble members to contribute greatly to the process yet keep them on track toward a larger vision. Articulating the vision is the director's first step toward attaining it.

If we start from the assumption that every script is open to a variety of interpretations, the director's primary responsibility could be defined as articulating a particular vision for a single production of the play. One of the ways a director can keep his or her vision from becoming static or closed to varied audience interpretations is to empower the ensemble members to create freely within their spheres of responsibilities. In this view, the director is more like a conductor: there is a score (the text), and the director's interpretation, but the musicians will try to contribute their own ideas to the melding of the score, the director's vision, and the playing of the orchestra (in theater, the ensemble). More creative voices can add depth and what can be constructive thematic ambiguity, so long as the director keeps this ambiguity from spinning out of control. A collaborative director therefore seeks a balance between ambiguity and clarity, individual creativity and cohesiveness. By working this way, you seek to take full advantage of the ensemble's talents. After all, in the end, the actors should know their characters better than the director, just as the designers should know their designs better than the director, because everyone but the director will spend more time and energy on his or her part of the production than the director, who is responsible for the entire production. A more authoritarian directing style might not always allow or encourage these kinds of contributions. Admittedly, many prominent directors attempt to retain power over the details within each area of production. A number of directors have followed the more authoritarian model successfully, although most can't do so because they lack the visual skills of a strong designer or the interpretive skills of an experienced actor.[1] Even those directors who have these skills at their disposal can benefit from the more focused and specialized attention that members of the ensemble can bring to their respective responsibilities. Opening the door to collaboration allows the ensemble to contribute skills and ideas, increasing the tools in your directing toolbox. But if the director learns to trust the ensemble to make strong interpretative contributions to the production, then what exactly is the director's responsibility within the ensemble? What must the director do to define and focus the production for the ensemble so that everyone can work constructively toward the same end?

---

[1]Theater directors like Robert Wilson and Peter Sellars are often labeled "*auteur* directors," a term borrowed from film theory but used within theater to describe directors who are heavily conceptual and display a consistent and recognizable style. Although both of these directors are quite accomplished, work like this requires the director to have extraordinary skills as a visual artist, or at the very least, extraordinary vision as a theatrical artist.

The Core Action

The director's primary responsibility is for the "big picture." The idea of a central focus point for the production is so fundamental to the production's success that it is essential for us to define it before we proceed. Focus on keeping all collaborators on track to this goal, the **core action**, different from the term "action," which has varied meanings in different contexts.

Actors use the term "action" to describe what they are doing to another character in any given scene. In this context, action is a verb that captures or explores what one character is doing to the other character(s) at any given moment. (For more on the actor's approach to action, see "Actions and Objectives" in Chapter 4.) Playwrights and dramaturgs use the term "action" to describe the through-line of the plot: what fuels the engine of the play so that it has momentum, which might be the plot, the change in a character or group, or progression of places, sounds, and sights, for example. We will be using the term "core action" to unify the actor's understanding of action with the playwright's concept of action as an overall engine for the production that embraces textual and visceral elements, which therefore also includes the designers' notion of stage action. In our context, then, "action" is what moves the play, and it is "core" because the action centers or grounds what we see, hear, and otherwise perceive on stage.

Professional directors and designers might use other terms to describe this idea; the two most frequently used are *production concept* and **spine**. *Concept* has several strikes against it as a useful term, however. First, it is a static word, somewhat akin to "theme," and thus it frequently yields productions that are about something—a unifying idea—but lack motion or a sense of progression. Second, it is a somewhat abstract word that erects a hurdle between the idea and its achievement: How do we put a concept on stage and make it compelling? Third, "concept" has been conflated with the term "concept production," which has gotten a bit of a bad name over the past few decades as an umbrella for heavy directorial decision making, such as when a director sets a production in a setting radically different from what the playwright calls for or reconstructs the script for a new purpose.

The term "spine," although more precise, suffers from some of the same problems. The late Harold Clurman, co-founder of the Group Theater, used the word "spine" to indicate the "chief motivating action" of a play. Yet the word is still somewhat static, and its anatomical origins complicate its utility. The human spine has a fairly regular shape, a double curve, and although disease might cause someone's spine to deviate from a regular shape, a spine functions in certain ways. Of course, "spine" may also be used to describe the center of a book binding, but most if not all meanings of this word share one element: Spines are somewhat rigidly constructed. For this reason, although Clurman's use of the word works well for plays that use traditional, linear narratives, "spine" does not work as well as a term for describing plays and narratives that deviate from linear forms. "Core action," which blends the textual and the visceral and leaves open the shape the action might take in any given production, is preferable.

Chapter 2 defines core action in greater detail, but for now we can start with the idea that the core action of a play is what drives it or, more accurately, what the director chooses as the "engine" for a particular production. If the director clearly defines the core action and keeps the ensemble on track toward that common goal or vision, then the production has a good chance of succeeding.

A director thus leads a production by defining its goals through the core action, and a good choice motivates the total ensemble to create the details that complete the action and give it a shape and style that make sense within its own logic. I say "its own logic" because for many years the view of what makes the different parts of a production work together has been "unity" or "coherence." These terms denote a certain type of logic that a large number of audience members would or could accept. Frequently, unity is achieved through the narrative; if the production can clearly tell an agreed-upon story, it will possess a certain type of unity. The problem here is twofold: (1) not all good plays or productions are primarily narrative-driven, and (2) a clear narrative is not, in and of itself, enough to make a production compelling. "Core action" is better than "narrative" because it covers less traditional plays and productions, which might be fueled by elements other than narrative. We will explore this notion in the following chapters.

As the director, you should be able to describe the core action of the play in one to three sentences or even a few key words, as well as expand your description to encompass all elements of production. Being able to be succinct about action helps focus the ensemble, but it requires you to be more exacting in your choice of words. Action is what advances the play—often plot, but not solely or under all circumstances, as in many avant-garde and absurdist plays. You should look for what moves the play forward and then describe this action in a way that stimulates the ensemble to create a production together.

The director must give the action, once defined, a shape. Think of shape as including all the elements of production, from acting and music to rhythm and tempo to colors and textures. Your collaboration should aim to achieve a compelling and clear shape that communicates your vision most effectively. If you have a clear grasp of the action and shape (what some directors refer to as the "arc" of the play), you need not have the answer to every question about the play at your fingertips. The definition of the action will help you lead the ensemble to make effective choices. In a pinch, you can refer to the action and shape of the overall production as a guide for evaluating choices and suggestions during the process, stimulating new ideas, and contributing ideas of your own. It will frequently be easier to justify not using one of your collaborators' ideas about a particular moment in the play if you can refer to your original description of the core action. If the action is your primary focus, you can make choices about whether to use each ensemble member's contributions with action as your guide and justification.

Emphasizing action as the ensemble's shared starting point for its work helps keep the work environment constructive. Try to avoid using emotionally charged negatives when you turn down someone's idea, as this tends to stigmatize the idea (as well as your cast member or designer) and might discourage the ensemble from taking further risks. Instead, you can say, "That's a bold choice, and I'm glad we tried it, but I don't think it fits the overall aim of this production." Similarly, you can try and then reject your own ideas with this justification, saying to the cast or designers, "I wanted to try that, but now I see that it doesn't support the vision we're all working toward." By trying and rejecting your own ideas according to the same rules as those for any other ensemble member's, you build an environment based on trust. In such an environment, risk taking becomes second nature, trying and rejecting ideas becomes a constructive way to discover what the play or production could be, and the larger definition of the core action helps you lead. If you reach this ideal with your ensemble, you need only keep everyone working together toward that goal, evaluating choices and shaping what the total ensemble creates.

The Responsibilities of Collaboration

What, then, are the boundaries between the director's responsibilities and those of the rest of the ensemble? Compare the artists who create theater with architects and builders: The director is the architect, but he or she might build the production using a variety of materials. As director, you in essence subcontract parts of the project to the ensemble. The blueprint that you will describe—the core action and its shape—might be achieved in many different ways, depending upon the people with whom you are working and the skills and materials at their disposal. This is why casting and selecting designers and staff are so important to the project. Keep your eyes on the overall "building," but don't try to be a specialist in every area of construction. The actors should know more about their characters than you do. The designers (when you reach the point in your career in which you have designers) should know more about design materials and approaches. Trust them, and you will encourage them to trust you. You can then select from the ideas generated within the ensemble to create the desired shape. The more the ensemble members feel that the director is listening to them and allowing them to contribute, the more they will feel that they are a vital part of the production. Productions gain energy and momentum from this confidence, commitment, and sense of ownership.

Dramaturgs and technical staff are, by the nature of their roles (in the American theater, at any rate), a bit more difficult to incorporate fully into the ensemble. In the United States, the role of the dramaturg is many faceted and ill defined. Professional and academic theaters frequently struggle to integrate dramaturgs successfully. In the professional theater, dramaturgs most often serve as literary managers; production dramaturgs are less common and tend to be under-used. In colleges and universities, the role of the production dramaturg, if there is one, is poorly defined as well.

Ideally, a dramaturg should function as a second set of critical eyes, someone who has done extensive research on the play, the playwright, the writing and world of the play, and its genre, for example, so that he or she can critique the work in progress. Very few theater programs fully use a production dramaturg, instead having them write program notes or research obscure minutiae about the play. Many academic theaters do not train or use dramaturgs. Frequently, directors do their own dramaturgical work. Avail yourself of the opportunity to work with an insightful dramaturg if given the opportunity; it can be an inexpensive, invaluable addition to the collaborative process.

The ensemble depends upon stage managers, board operators, and backstage crews to establish and execute a good portion of the rhythm of the production; build crews construct performance space, which will serve as the world of the play. The technical staff tends to be divided from the larger ensemble because of the lack of contact between technical staff and the cast and infrequent contact (often limited to production meetings) between the director and the staff. By the nature of their jobs, technical staff members tend to work primarily with the designers and crews. I know of no easy answers to these problems, but I will suggest a few things that might help directors include as many people in the overall collaboration as possible. For instance, invite the entire staff of the production to the first cast meeting and design presentations as part of a "meet-and-greet" get-together. Opening rehearsals to staff and crew at particular points in the process not only increases their contact with the cast, but also frequently results in conversations about how the production will function pragmatically. The primary duty of the director in this regard is to stay in touch with everyone working on the production, treat everyone with respect, and set up an atmosphere in which respect is the norm. This is one of the essential times for the director to lead by example. If you, as director, treat everyone with respect, others are more likely to do the same. Everyone in a production adds to the working atmosphere and feelings of commitment and pride. Effort and expertise deserve gratitude and respect, and your ensemble will follow your lead if you make your appreciation known. As with designers and actors, technical staff members should know their jobs better than the director, and that entitles them to everyone's respect.

Fundamental Techniques

All exercises in this book are based on collaboration and/or experiential (or active) learning. The exercises provide a series of challenges for you to solve. There is rarely a single solution to any given production challenge and, similarly, there are no "correct answers" to these exercises. The goal is for you to experiment and develop several possible solutions and then learn by analyzing and discussing them. Once experienced, the class critiques the work, isolating key concepts from students' discoveries. At the end of each chapter, we'll review the key concepts in brief, so that you can solidify what you've learned and link concepts and terminology to your experiences. Particularly in the first half of the book, many of the exercises are designed for teams of two or more, with no single person leading; each team will attempt to arrive at the strongest and most interesting choices while staying true to individual visions or discovering an even stronger shared vision.

To improve your ability to collaborate, the book requires you to work on many of the early directing exercises in pairs, with both students working simultaneously as actor and director on a scene from a play that the whole class works on at the same time. Each of you will come up with your own vision for a short scene before class and rehearsal; the rehearsal process consists of melding the two directors' visions by every means of communication available, among them blocking, reciprocal action, and character arcs, all based upon each person's evolving interpretation of the scene and play.

- **Role-playing exercises** involve students working in groups of two or three with identifiable jobs and sometimes "characters" to play. Your instructor may watch or join in. Role-playing exercises allow students to experience and observe a wide range of situations that they might encounter as directors before they begin directing their final projects.
- **Simulation exercises** involve the entire class at once in an exercise based on a set of rules, but without set characters to play. For example, a simulated audition might help you learn how to audition actors. Simulations allow you to try different techniques, observe and borrow successful techniques from each other, and gain a feeling of experience and comfort in a situation before you experience the real thing.
- **Writing-to-learn exercises** involve the use of ungraded writing assignments and written, in-class dialogues to explore the central ideas of the directing course. These exercises may consist of journals, short papers written outside class, or in-class writing assignments. "Writing to learn" does not involve students' displaying their knowledge through their writing, as in traditional "term papers," but learning through writing itself. Because many of these assignments can be ungraded, you can focus on writing as a way to express ideas and communicate with classmates—invaluable skills for directors that transfer well beyond the classroom.
- Many of the writing exercises introduced in this book involve **team writing**, in which small groups of two or three attempt to come to a consensus on a directing issue, such as the key moment in a scene or play. By doing these exercises in written form, you work on the clarity of your written expression, since you cannot rely on verbal skills to make up for ambiguous writing. The pressure many students feel to "write well" gives way to a genuine desire to communicate ideas, frequently resulting in more persuasive writing. Subsequent discussion can be used to clarify communication, as

well as provide constructive feedback on both the process and the product of the writing exercise.

Here are some initial exercises to get you to try to collaborate and solve problems together:

1. Working in groups of three or four, select a short poem or section of a poem and stage it as an ensemble. Each group should aim to reach agreement on an interpretation and be able to support its choices with references to the text. Make concrete choices about movement, rhythm, and space, and find, explore, or impose a structure on the poem. After all the pieces have been performed, discuss the following issues:
    a. What was the connection between the staging and the text?
    b. How did the group arrive at consensus? How did the process benefit or hinder the product?
    c. What choices did your group make about movement, rhythm, and space? What choices seemed to occur naturally through the process of working on the piece?
    d. What were the keys to the structure of the staging?

2. Working from a painting, photograph, or other visual image, create a staging based on or in reaction to the image, working in groups of three or four. Aim for the best interpretation that all members of the group can support. The staging need not be a literal translation of the image, but one that reflects upon or reacts to its moods, colors, structure, rhythm, or style. After viewing all the pieces, write down your individual reactions before discussing them with your group or the class:
    a. Is responding to a nontextual source easier or harder than staging a text? How does it differ?
    b. What issues arise in working toward consensus? What was difficult about this process?
    c. Was each piece coherent? What gave it coherence? What did it seem to be about? Aside from narrative, what makes a staging seem "complete"?

3. Try either of the above exercises with five minutes of individual preparation before the group works together. Each person should aim to actualize something significant from his or her interpretation while responding to and working with the other members' ideas. After viewing all the pieces, write down your reactions to the following issues, and then discuss them as a group or class:
    a. How does the process differ when each ensemble member comes to the process with ideas?
    b. Was it easier or harder to collaborate when each person brought ideas into the process?

c. What would you keep if you continued to work on this piece? What would you do differently if you had ultimate authority over the process and product?

d. How much did other people's ideas change or add to your original conception for the piece?

Our focus will be on how to use analysis as the basis for collaboration, as a springboard for opening the play to several interpretations rather than a method of narrowing those interpretations and the choices that may be used to achieve them. In Chapter 4, you will work on exercises focusing on the visceral elements of production (composition, blocking, tempo, rhythm, and so on) and others focusing on textual elements traditionally thought of as part of script analysis (dramatic structure, action/objective, relationships, and the like). These exercises can be alternated to encourage the integration of textual and visceral elements and break down the barrier between the parts of the director's job that are frequently deemed intellectual or analytical and the parts that are considered more creative or intuitive. After these exercises, I have included a summary to solidify the analytic concepts and prepare you to communicate your overall "take" on a play, in both written and oral form, to the ensemble. Read this section any time in your study with this book; indeed, rereading the section on analysis throughout the course should yield new insights into the purpose and use of script analysis.

Another central tenet of the book is that directing is about limits—those we place on ourselves as theater artists as well as our ability to develop within and beyond them. Most directing decisions, whether arrived at through collaboration or directorial fiat, involve placing limits on a production: setting a production in a particular period or place; performing a play in a particular space or configuration; directing actors in a particular style; selecting a central image, arc, throughline, or color palette. The budget for your production will almost always place limitations on what you can do on stage. For your first productions, you will be creating theater with little or no money at all. This is sometimes called "poor theater," which we'll discuss in more detail in Chapter 3. Rather than view the limitations of the medium in which we are working as confining, I encourage you to start from the assumption that *limitations create opportunities for artistic expression.* Having less—less money, less technical support, fewer physical resources— pushes us to be more creative. For example, the convention that a theater audience remains stationary during the performance can stimulate directors to work creatively within this limitation, or to work beyond it, by moving the audience through the space during the performance. Through active learning exercises, you will explore attempts to work within, and try to overcome, limitations, and to seek creative solutions that transform limitations into new creative solutions—a mark of a true theater artist.

The director is the central character in a performance that is called the rehearsal, yet the director should not bring attention to this fact. Too little attention is paid to the director's presence in rehearsal and the effect of his or her interaction with the ensemble. The director should be a "stealth actor" in each rehearsal. For example, the director should be attuned to the impact of his or her own physical actions in the rehearsal, rather than seeing himself or herself as a talking head or "pure mind." Where the director sits or stands, what tone of voice he or she uses, whether he or she touches the actors, where he or she stands in relation to the actors are all elements of the director's performance and may be used as tools of communication. But the director should not be a scene-stealer. In rehearsal, as in life, how we say or do something communicates as much as, if not more than, what we actually say. Within this rubric, I suggest ways in which rehearsal observations and videotape can be used to critique the directors' "performances."

We will use Harold Pinter's *Betrayal* as the central example for analysis and the play text for the first directing exercises, although other scripts may be substituted. The text is valuable for us because of Pinter's facility with playable dialogue and conflict, his use of ambiguity to create subtexts that remain open to a variety of interpretations, and for the unique dramatic structure of the text, which goes backward and forward in time. Particularly in the Internet age, time and structure seem less linear and more fluid, thus the structure of the play seems particularly accessible to contemporary students. On a scene-by-scene level, *Betrayal* is essentially realistic, which makes it ideal for a first directing scene because the core actions of the scenes are more available to developing directors. The nonrealistic structure of the play, however, forces directors to deal with the difference between the action of the chronological story and the sequence of events the playwright has chosen. By selecting when the play goes backward and forward, Pinter forces us to find the nonchronological arc for the characters, the scenes, and the play. The play consists of nine two- and three-person scenes, it is easy to cast for the gender makeup of most classes. Should more scenes for actresses be needed, you can supplement it with scenes from Pinter's *Old Times* (or other plays by Pinter and others) from the same Pinter anthology.

SUPPLEMENTAL READING

Chinoy, Helen K. Introduction to *Directors on Directing*, edited by Toby Cole and Helen K. Chinoy. Rev. ed. Indianapolis: Bobbs Merrill, 1963.
Clurman, Harold. *On Directing*. New York: Macmillan, 1972.
Fink, L. Dee. *Creating Significant Learning Experiences*. San Francisco: Jossey-Bass, 2003.
Soven, Margot K. *Write to Learn: Guide to Writing across the Curriculum*. Cincinnati: South-Western College, 1996.

CHAPTER

1

Collaboration and Leadership

The collaborative director is, as Robert Cohen and John Harrop put it in their book *Creative Play Direction*, "first among equals." In essence, he or she seeks to lead the ensemble through a constructive process toward a product (the production) that achieves the director's overall interpretation of the script. To do so, the director aims for a type of collaboration that works best for the production and the ensemble. The director must use his or her judgment and appraisal of the ensemble members' skills and personalities to find the best collaborative process, which will vary from show to show. It is not my purpose to dictate a specific collaborative process or relationship, but to help you develop the range and depth of your collaborative skills. Once you have begun to acquire these skills, your challenge will be to find a working balance between collaboration and leadership—a valuable skill, whether in theater or life. Collaboration without leadership tends to degenerate into chaos, unless the ensemble already embraces a shared aesthetic, social, or political aim. Most people like to feel that they are accomplishing something, and someone must define that "something." In theater, the director defines where the play or production is going. This involves interpreting the script, the raw material of any production. Whether the playwright is dead or alive, absent or present, the director's interpretation starts with the script—the playwright's words. The director might collaborate with some or all of the ensemble members in defining the core of the production and bringing it to fruition, but ultimately the director makes the final decision as to the overall aim of the production.

Directors must set the boundaries of their jobs for each production. Clearly defining your responsibilities and those of your ensemble at the start of the process will help guide you. Let's start with the idea that the director is responsible for the "big picture" of the production. No matter how much artistic input you solicit from the ensemble, ultimately you are responsible for bringing together each individual's contribution so that it works with the rest of the ensemble and the big picture. By keeping your eyes on the "big picture" of the production, you may allow actors and designers much greater latitude to create within your overall interpretation of the script. Once you open the directing process to collaboration, though, how do you balance collaboration with leadership to achieve your aims?

Balancing Leadership and Collaboration

Perhaps the most frightening part of becoming a collaborative director is the loss of control that this approach appears to necessitate. After all, many theater artists, particularly directors, see their productions as an extension of themselves, and they want their work to look a certain way—the way they have envisioned it. The artistic control that a director enjoys (or imagines) can be heady stuff. If we view one of the primary jobs of the director as creating a world, then the director can be seen as the creator of this world, albeit based loosely or closely on the words of the playwright. That is exactly why the director needs to share responsibility for the production with his or her collaborators. No director knows the best way to achieve every detail within this world. The best directors welcome and encourage constructive contributions. Yet many people find it difficult at first to direct in a collaborative way, since it requires the director to sacrifice a certain amount of artistic control.

The director must develop certain skills to work in this way. Verbal and written communication, script analysis, visual aesthetics, and some knowledge of how each member of the total ensemble works serve as the foundation for collaboration. The first three enable the director to understand and interpret the script and communicate this vision to the ensemble. The fourth, understanding how everyone else in the ensemble works, might take a while to acquire. To be truly effective, a director must understand how actors, designers, writers, dramaturgs, stage managers, and technical staff work to communicate with other ensemble members and evaluate their ideas knowledgeably. If you become serious about directing, you need to acquire basic skills in each of these areas. As a developing director, you should first acquire or expand your knowledge of acting. As you direct more, always try to supplement this work with study and work in all areas of theater.

To grow as a director requires continual study and experimentation, not only as a director, but also in other areas of theater and other disciplines. Push yourself to go beyond your perceived limits; direct plays outside your favorite periods and styles; take classes or workshops in acting, design, playwriting, music, and art history, particularly if these are weak points for you; see theater created in every imaginable style, theater space, and type of ensemble. Otherwise you risk repeating yourself and becoming bored. In the film *Annie Hall,* Woody Allen's character, Alvey Singer, talks to Annie about why their relationship isn't working out, and his words are easily applied to the relationship between directors and their work: "A relationship, I think, is like a shark. You know? It has to constantly move forward or it dies. And I think what we got on our hands is a dead shark." Point taken: As a director, grow or die.

The goal, therefore, is not only to help you acquire collaborative directing techniques but to expand your capacity for growth as a director, for collaborators influence directors and productions greatly. By learning to collaborate well, directors develop their interpersonal skills, make themselves more desirable and marketable, and continue their growth as artists. By being open to the ideas of collaborators, the director opens the door to new ideas for the current production and learns techniques for future productions.

What does it mean for a collaborative director to be a good leader? If the director wants to work collaboratively and avoid telling everyone what to do, how can he or she lead a production effectively? One way to begin to understand how you can lead and collaborate effectively is to look at the approaches available to you as a director and explore how they further leadership and/or collaboration.

EXERCISE

Examine the following skills and functions that a director might serve. Working on your own, divide the list under two headings: leadership and collaboration. Put the items into whichever category you think they further most. If you find that the item fits both categories equally, include it in both lists. In smaller groups of two to four, discuss your choices and try to come to a consensus. Finally, discuss your group's answers with the class as a whole.

> Balancing idealism and pragmatism
> Confidence and dependability
> Defining and reaching goals
> Energizing the ensemble
> Keeping order
> Listening to others' ideas
> Making choices
> Mediating conflict
> Redirecting focus
> Respecting others

Some of you might be able to place these skills and qualities neatly into the two categories of leadership and collaboration. Others might find that many of these terms fall into both categories. There is no single correct answer to this exercise because it depends upon how you employ these skills as much as how you define and understand them.

Now that you have discussed these terms, I will provide you with my responses to what the terms mean and why they are important to directors. I will start with the terms that seem to emphasize collaboration:

- **Energizing the ensemble**. The director fuels the energies of ensemble members so they give their utmost to the production. To do this, you should be willing to try everyone's ideas, as time permits, to say yes and give credit when other people pitch ideas and they work, and to say no even to your own ideas when they don't work. By rejecting your own ideas and showing a willingness to fail boldly, you can set an example for others. Try to offer one outlandish idea early in the rehearsal process and let it fail, so that you can shrug it off without embarrassment. It's a way of giving permission to the cast and to you to fail, with the knowledge that failure is a small price to pay for the knowledge that bold risk taking might help you discover.

- **Balancing idealism and pragmatism**. Directors are, by nature, idealists. To direct is to wish to create a world on stage perfectly. But perfect worlds don't exist on stage for very long; we're lucky if we create a few perfect moments within an imaginative, if occasionally flawed, world. We strive for the ideal, and the director must inspire the ensemble's hunger for the ideal, but eventually reality hits. The director must learn to balance the ideal with the pragmatic.

- **Respecting others**. It is in the best interests of the ensemble and the production for the director to set an example by showing respect for everyone's work. This means that the director should listen to new ideas, try them whenever practical, and strive to treat everyone with respect, even under the most stressful circumstances. Because so many people give so much time and energy to a production, everyone in the ensemble deserves respect. In the heat of the moment, this principle might inadvertently be sacrificed, but it is your responsibility to create an atmosphere of respect and to help reestablish it when it is broken.

- **Listening to others' ideas**. Listening to the ideas of others not only helps the director create an atmosphere of respect, but also displays confidence in the director's own ideas. If your idea is truly the best solution, an open discussion of the alternatives should only reinforce the strength of your decision. At the same time, you might discover new things about the play or scene through discussing or trying alternatives. You have the final decision-making power, so you can afford to be open to other ideas.

Another set of these terms emphasizes leadership, but these leadership qualities are necessary to achieve strong collaboration. The director's leadership in certain areas of the production process helps create the environment for collaboration. These qualities develop the ensemble's focus, a precursor for sharing ideas and working together:

- **Making choices**. The director must be willing and able to make choices about all aspects of the production, from the artistic (acting, design, dramaturgy) to the practical (rehearsal schedules, production meetings). Regardless of how much input the director encourages the ensemble to provide, the director eventually makes decisions about most elements of the production. Indecisive directing is not collaboration. On the contrary, collaborative directing usually requires the director to make many strong decisions. The more ideas your ensemble develops, the more decisions you'll have to make. Through preparation, analysis, and judgment, the director should be prepared to make these choices. The better prepared the director is going into the rehearsal and design process, the easier it will be to explain choices rationally. Rational explanations of choices foster respect and confidence.

■ **Defining and reaching goals**. The director must define the goals of the production and of each rehearsal or meeting clearly. No other person in the ensemble has this power, and if the director doesn't perform this function, then the process will drift. Setting periodic goals helps ensemble members believe in the director's vision; reaching goals gives everyone a feeling of confidence about how the production is progressing. Yet some of your collaborators might respond to different approaches than others. Some theater artists need space to experiment, whereas others need step-by-step guidance. Reaching goals can and should involve collaboration as well: the ability to adjust your approach to the artists you are working with and respond to their ideas as well as their needs.

■ **Keeping order**. The director keeps the total ensemble working productively and on schedule. Some members of the ensemble will naturally be more meticulous about deadlines than others. The single most important factor in encouraging all members of the ensemble to contribute creatively in a timely manner is your own behavior. Lead by example; your discipline will encourage others to follow. If you provide a sloppy example, the production will follow a far riskier course.

■ **Redirecting focus**. There are many times when the rehearsal or design process strays from its primary purpose: when an idea takes the production away from the core action or common goal; when ensemble members become overly concerned with product too early in the process; when a cast gets giddy. The director's responsibility is to redirect the focus of the ensemble in these circumstances, so that its members return to constructive work without any loss in confidence or self-esteem.

■ **Mediating conflict**. All directors wish for the creative process to go without a hitch, but this rarely occurs. We all bring outside baggage into rehearsal, we don't always like each other, and sometimes we're simply tired. As a member of the ensemble, the director is as prone to these pitfalls as anyone else. But the director has a special responsibility to monitor the process and to mediate conflicts when they arise. This means checking in with your ensemble members periodically, watching ensemble interactions for signs of conflict, and keeping an eye on your own behavior. Never get so wrapped up in the moment that you lose track of the atmosphere of the process.

■ **Confidence and dependability**. A good director is confident, inspires confidence, and encourages it in others. A confident ensemble performs to the best of its abilities. The same goes for dependability. You must be meticulous in your work habits if you intend to ask the same from your ensemble. Come to rehearsal early, be prepared for all meetings and rehearsals, and follow through on all promises. If you set this kind of example, the ensemble is more likely to follow your lead.

DISCUSSION QUESTIONS

In small groups of two to four, discuss some or all of the following questions. Reach a consensus on the most important aspects of the group's answer to each question. When each group has reached a consensus, reassemble as a large group to share and discuss the answers.

1. What choices is a director responsible for? What circumstances change the answer to this question?

2. How does a director know when to continue to strive for the ideal and when to compromise?

3. How can a director inspire the ensemble to do their best work?

4. What strategies should a director employ in mediating conflict? What strategies should be avoided?

5. What are your strongest personal qualities as a director? What areas do you need to work on?

SUPPLEMENTAL READING

Cohen, Robert, and John Harrup. *Creative Play Direction.* Englewood Cliffs, NJ: Prentice-Hall, 1984.
Daniels, Rebecca. *Women Stage Directors Speak: Exploring the Influence of Gender on Their Work.* Jefferson, NC: McFarland, 1996.
Fisher, Roger, William Ury, and Bruce Patton. *Getting to Yes: Negotiating Agreement without Giving In.* 2nd ed. London: Penguin, 1991.

CHAPTER

2

Core Action

Next to casting, choosing the core action is the single most important thing a director does. In every production, a director makes some choices about the core action, and no one choice is the only "correct" one; if there were only one answer to this central question, directing would be solely craft. Although the craft of directing—the nuts and bolts of putting a play on its feet—is an essential part of the director's work, the art of directing—the director's interpretation of the script and the creation of its new life on stage—is equally essential to effective theater. No matter how specific the playwright's notes and stage directions are, the director has the responsibility for choosing the core action for his or her particular production. Scripts are made up of words in a particular order, yet these words reveal a range of interpretations of the action. The choices that you and your ensemble make will bring out different aspects of any play. Without something to guide you and your ensemble in making these choices, you will find it difficult to lead and your ensemble will find it hard to bring their work together into a cohesive whole. Your aim, therefore, is to capture something vital to the script and spark the ensemble to create and expand upon it. To reiterate, the core action of a play is the director's sense of what drives the play, a combination of the actors' actions, the playwright's intentions, the space, the language, rhythm, and tempo. The core action finds its form in all the textual and visceral elements of the production; it simultaneously leads and is shaped by the artistic choices of the entire ensemble.

Story and Plot

Most theater practitioners and scholars agree on a basic distinction between story and plot drawn from Aristotle's definition of plot in his *Poetics* (350 B.C.). **Story** is the sum of all narrative facts that occur or are alluded to in the text. Story includes not only all the events that occur on stage, but also all the events that occur offstage, as well as past events discussed or implied during the play. **Plot** is the playwright's selection and arrangement of events for portrayal on stage. Story is chronological, whereas plot follows the playwright's logic for the drama, how he or she wishes to see events unfold. Plot is what actually happens on stage, whereas story includes every event that the play or characters refer to, even if it is not shown on stage.

"Action," however, is a much more loosely defined term, most concretely referred to in writings about acting. Within most of the systems of acting based on Stanislavski's acting theories, "action" refers to the verb that an actor uses to play a scene or moment. Actors see scenes in terms of action and objective, and the action is the verb—what their character is doing to the other character (we will examine the actor's use of actions and objectives in detail in the next chapter). Directors are usually intimately involved in the actors' choices of actions, as these are among a director's strongest interpretative tools. Just as the actor must experiment and eventually decide upon his or her character's actions from moment to moment, the director must find the action of the play from scene to scene or unit to unit.

In the following chapters, you will work on developing the depth and range of your analytic tools by looking at a full-length play from a variety of points of view: character, composition, blocking, and so on. At this point, it is not necessary for you to embark upon a complete script analysis; you should focus solely on finding or choosing the core action of a short play. After you have read the play below once or twice, work in groups on the exercises that follow. For now, complete the exercises without any dramaturgical background, other than to note that Laurence Klavan, an American playwright, wrote the play in 2002.

The New Rules

by Laurence Klavan

A nondescript waiting area. Two chairs, two men. #1, a hail-fellow type, enters and addresses #2, who's twitching and traumatized.

#1:   This seat taken?

> *#2 nods, then shakes his head, then shrugs. Then #1 can see he's just shaking in general. So he sits down.*

#1:   So. Haven't been here for a while . . . I've been away. See my skin tone? See my tan? I've been outside. (*Looks around*) Not the same old place here, I'm surprised to say. Fresh coat of paint, or something.

> *Far gone, #2 doesn't respond.*

#1:   Not the neighborliest man, are you?

> *Then—*

#1:   Oh. Oh. I'm sorry. It's silly of me. I stepped away for a second, and simply forgot. Something's just happened, hasn't it?

> *#2 shakes his head.*

#1:   Don't try to talk. It's okay. I understand.

#2:   (*Managing to speak*) No, you don't.

#1:   You so sure? How come? What's new?

#2:   Nothing's happened for months.

#1:   What do you mean?

#2:   It's the new rules.

#1:   (*Beat.*) What do you mean? There's no longer—

#2:   Any specific time that—

#1:   You know something's going to happen?

#2:   Right.

#1:   My God. I mean, before, you know, you could prepare—you could set a place on the table inside yourself, so to say. You knew that, every Tuesday at two—

#2:   Or Friday at four, that was my—

#1:   You would be made to walk through the maze, and then be tied down upon a table—

#2:   Or in a chair, take your choice—

#1:   Hooked up—

#2:   Attached, exactly—

#1:   —to a machine, and made to look at yourself in the mirror while you were shot through with thousands of volts of electricity—

#2:   —which lasted just long enough for your body to start to burn—

#1:   —for the smoke from your skin to start to—yes, that was the buzzer, that was the bell—

#2:   —that meant you could then weave your way back through the maze—

#1:   —if you could—or simply crawl—

#2:   —see, I could go home, that was why the Friday.

#1:   Fine. And it was accepted. On Tuesday, I knew I would take two sharp rights, go through a small swinging door, and experience eye-popping pain. The pattern was—

#2:   Healthy.

#1:   In the end, yes, that's what was proved, according to the experts. We had the same level of stress, in the end, as those who were exempt, as the Variables. And has anyone ever met a Variable? Do they even exist? Is there anyone who hasn't, at one time or another, been electrocuted?— Is it an inherited position, some sort of Civil Service job, where—

#2:   Cut it out, for Chrissake.

#1:   But to have these new rules, where you'll never know when you'll be shocked—when you'll suffer—to have it always be a surprise, to live always in suspense—that kind of anxiety can't be good for the . . . well, you're a case in point.

>   *Twitching, #2 looks over.*

#2:   Yes, I guess I am. And you're already on your way, too, now, aren't you?

>   *#1 looks at him. Then, freaked, jumping up.*

#1:   You know, wait a—I'll be back in just a—I think I left my comb back in the—

#2:   Don't bother. There's no way back. You can only go ahead from here, and now the maze is much more twisty.

#1:   What? Now, hold on here—give me those random dates, and I'll perceive a pattern—my mind is fresh, I'm well-rested—and maybe you're not so good at math—

#2:   (*Takes out tiny little crumples of paper*) I'm an accountant for a king, but hey, feel free to . . .

#1:   (*Sees the crumples; then—*) Hey, who's in charge here? The same kind of crew? Everyone was always so impressed, but they weren't so tough. I'll just give them a piece of my mind, and—

#2:   It's a new group. There are so many more now. And if you thought they were big before . . .

>   *The sound of a giant rat is heard scurrying from left to center. The two men freeze. Silence. Then the rat is heard scurrying from center to right.*

#1:   Jesus Christ. Now I know what they mean by nostalgia.

>   *But #2 is even more agitated, twitching over on his side on his chair.*

#1:   Hey—hey—are you all right?

#2:   Yes—yes—nothing happened. Don't you see? Nothing happened again. I feel just . . . fine.

>   *He stops moving. Slowly, #1 takes his pulse. He's dead. Horrified, #1 backs off.*

#1:   Oh no . . . (*looking around, frantically*) help! Help!

>   *But it is obvious no help will come. Then, swallowing deeply, he calls to those above him.*

#1:   Hey! Hey! Don't you have any decency? Can't you see what you're doing now?

Shocked, he falls to his knees.

#1:   Please . . . please . . . I'm begging you . . . Don't make me end up like him. Look, I'll make you a deal. I'll do whatever you want . . . If you'll only . . . if you'll only promise . . . if you'll only promise to . . . hurt me.

Blackout

© Copyright 2002, Laurence Klavan. For information on production rights for *The New Rules*, please contact Ron Gwiazda, Rosenstone/Wender, 38 E. 29th St., 10th floor, New York, NY 10016. Email: Rosenstone@aol.com

EXERCISE

In teams of two, discuss some of the following questions one at a time. Be sure to answer question 7 on the core action. Spend five to ten minutes arriving at and writing your answers individually, and then exchange your answers with your partner. Pass the answers back and forth until you reach a consensus on the most important aspects of your answer. Be prepared to justify your choices with evidence from the text, but try to be receptive to your partner's choices. When each team has reached a consensus or an impasse, reassemble as a large group to share and discuss your answers.

1. What is the most important line in the play?
2. What is the most important sound in the play?
3. What is the most important moment in the play?
4. What is the most important rule in this world?
5. Where and when is the play set?
6. What are the differences between the two characters?
7. What is the core action of the play?

Exercise Critique

Discuss the choices each team has made.

- Did every team make the same choices? If not, what are the implications for each choice in production? Do some team's choices seem more aggressive in their interpretation of the script? Does the text justify the choices?
- How do questions 1–7 above relate to the core action? What makes a statement of core action compelling?

In critiquing your work on the exercise, look at both the process and the product. For process: Did you accept good ideas from your partner? Were you able to convince your partner of the validity of your answers? Were you able to reach a consensus with which you and your partner both felt comfortable? Did the collaboration strengthen the consensus? What would you do differently to improve the collaboration? For product: Was your team's final version of core action for the play strong, inspiring, and connected to the text? Does it leave room for future collaborators to contribute to the project?

One director might see this as a play about two people terrorized by anxiety about unseen, unrealized threats. Another might say this is a play about how a system or world creates terror where none actually exists. You might see this as a play about how one person tries to protect another from his or her fears. Each of these statements will suggest different choices by the ensemble and ultimately lead to a unique creation.

A Playwright's Intentions

The New Rules was written in reaction to the terrorist destruction of the World Trade Center and performed at Town Hall in New York City on the first anniversary of the attacks, as part of a theater marathon called *Brave New World*. The play was one of the few in the festival that didn't treat 9/11 naturalistically. I thought that such an atrocity required abstraction; reality wasn't enough. (Onstage or off, it almost never is.)

Initially, I was reluctant to write anything. Having been in the city during the attacks, I thought that it would be tasteless and presumptuous. Also, I had no political insights into them and, watching TV and reading the papers, I thought no one else did, either. All I knew were my own feelings and one feeling in particular: anxiety. How would I write a play about that?

Then I had an unrelated conversation with my girlfriend, Susan. She mentioned a study of rats that were zapped by electrodes in experiments. After being shocked on a certain schedule, they would become stable emotionally. Uncertainty about the time and place of the pain, however, would drive them crazy. I thought: that's how I feel living in New York City after 9/11, with its constant (at this writing, anyway) false alarms. It gave me a way into the play.

Two characters have grown used to being tortured at a certain time. Take away the routine and they start to collapse. Finally, the worst thing of all becomes a threat of pain without a follow-through. One dies from the stress; the other ends up begging for at least the consistency of hardship. This is their response to the "new rules" of our world. This little play became mine.

—Laurence Klavan, playwright

Laurence Klavan's plays have been produced at Ensemble Studio Theatre, Manhattan Punch Line, Actors Theatre of Louisville, Wilma Theater, and the Vineyard Theater.

On one level, the play speaks for itself, but on another level, understanding the dramaturgical background of the play—information about the writing of the play and its historical, critical, and cultural context—opens the play to broader or more specific interpretation. Among the plays written for the marathon, Klavan's piece was one of the few that did not mention or directly refer to the events of September 11. The play implicity draws a parallel between the characters' situation and that of the American public after the attacks, when the raising and lowering of "terror threat levels" from yellow to orange to red kept America on edge, always waiting for something that never happened, at least as of the writing of this book. When #2 dies, presumably from the stress of constant, indeterminate threats, Klavan dramatizes the toll taken by post-9/11 anxiety. It is thus a political play, though not necessarily a partisan one; a personal play that expresses the playwright's reaction to the endless threat of terrorism.

The playwright offers very little about the location of this play. "A nondescript waiting area" and "two chairs" are the only specific stage directions. We can infer a bit more from where #1 has been and how he reacts to returning to this place: "I've been away. See my skin tone? See my tan? I've been outside. (*Looks around*) Not the same old place here, I'm surprised to say. Fresh coat of paint, or something." The characters also talk about what their daily routine is like: "On Tuesday, I knew I would take two sharp rights, go through a small swinging door, and experience eye-popping pain" and their reactions to the off-stage presence of the "new group" in charge. But the playwright has chosen a "nondescript" environment, an important piece of information for the director. Is Klavan deliberately using the avant-garde technique of ambiguity—a world and set of characters with little history or specificity—and, if so, to what purpose? Or are there other interpretations of this choice? Either way, the director will have to come to some understanding of the significance of the play's environment.

Action Analysis

In describing the core action of any play, the director should keep in mind the following points:

> **Specificity**. The director's statement of the core action must be specific and detailed. Broad, general statements about theme do not help the total ensemble collaborate toward the same end. The director should polish his or her core action statement until it communicates the essence of the interpretation clearly and succinctly. The statement should not be so long as to lose the director's "audience" (the ensemble) or so short as to be vague or unclear.

> **Inspiration**. The director's statement of the core action aims to inspire the ensemble toward creative and committed choices. There is no objective test for what will inspire an ensemble. A director must strive to inspire the ensemble not only with the quality and originality of his or her vision of the play, but also with a clear and dynamic presentation, both in substance and style.

Centrality. The director's choice of the core action should be central to the progression of events in the play. It should fuel all the scenes in the play, not just some of them. If the action selected is truly central, you should be able to follow this action step by step through the play.

Textual evidence. A successful core action tends to be tied in some fundamental way to the text. In contemporary theater, many directors feel empowered to diverge from the text to some extent, particularly when directing classic plays. Regardless of the extent of this divergence, the director needs to understand and to be able to explain the relationship between the text and his or her production ideas.

Research support. Additional dramaturgical research about the writing of the play, the life and works of the playwright, the style of the play or production, the world of the play, or criticism of the play might support the core action. See the Script Analysis and Dramaturgy Checklist at the end of Chapter 4.

Script Analysis

Now that you have had a chance to analyze a short play for action and collaborate with partners on specifying the core action and stating it, let's summarize some of the key things to look for in finding the core of a play. These terms will help you ground your future work in some basic elements of script analysis without focusing solely on the script at an early stage. Script analysis is a valuable tool, but developing directors find that analysis frequently limits their creative and more intuitive responses. Instead, you should acquire script analysis skills in tandem with staging skills, so as to balance what is written with what the audience will see and hear. The following terms are not just elements of script analysis, but also focal points for the rehearsal process, for your ensemble to discover or to elaborate upon:

Events. Whether they are realistic or nonrealistic, mainstream or avant-garde, almost all plays can be seen as a series of events, linked or related to one another. In a realistic play, the relationship between these events is most frequently causal. One event leads to the next event and so on, creating a chain of events that hits a point—what many scholars call the "turning point"—at which the ending becomes inevitable. The play then moves quickly and inevitably toward its climax, the key moment in the play, in which the central questions that have fueled the journey from event to event are answered. Nonrealistic and avant-garde plays frequently play with or against the audience's expectation of causality. Yet they can also be seen as a collection of events, though these events might pile up, be scattered and seemingly random, or have a shape or logic all their own, rather than the more typical, linear narrative line of realistic or "well-made" plays.

When the director or the ensemble discovers the "key moment" in a play or scene, this can be used to structure choices about the previous and subsequent events in the scene. In his book *Backwards and Forwards,* David Ball articulates a method of script analysis based on the idea that the chain of events in a play can be seen most easily by working backward, looking at the climax first to trace the events back to their starting point. You can work with the major points of his approach. Start by finding what you see as the climax of any given scene or play and then begin to figure out its significance. Who are the main players in the climax? What happens to them at the key moment in the play? Work backward through the play to find the sequence of events leading to the key moment. Starting with the climax ensures that the pattern you isolate is central to the dramatic structure of the play.

Even though any playwright might have a sequence of events in mind as the major arc of a play, different productions might focus on or develop different strands of the action. These strands represent different "core actions," and each one might result in a quite different production. The focus of the play could change depending upon the circumstances of production: the company, the director, the space, the time, and the place; the politics, economics, and culture of the society or community for which it is being produced. One thing remains a constant, however: the climax gains more power if the journey of the action fuels it. By searching for the connection between his or her choice of the key moment or climax and the events that lead to it, the director can test a particular take on the play to see whether it fits with the causal (or deliberately acausal) series of events that the playwright has written. In this way, it is possible to tweak or even go against the playwright's original intentions but remain true to the events that the playwright irrefutably built into the play. Look for the key moment with your ensemble, make sense of the sequence of events, and you'll be ready to use the director's tools for shaping the action, which we will explore in the following chapter.

Character. Like action, character can be looked at backward. First, though, let's discuss briefly what we mean by "character." The word can refer to the *dramatis personae* in a play, yet its two most common uses can be captured best in these phrases: "That person *has* character" and "That person *is* a character." In the first phrase, "character" refers to the quality of the person's being or actions; in the second, "character" suggests that the person is unusual in some way. We will use both senses of the word. When we discuss whether someone has character—or, in a play, whether a character has character—we look at his or her actions and beliefs. Usually, we think that someone has character when we approve of his or her beliefs and he or she acts on them. When we say that someone is a character, we are usually judging the person against the norms of his or her world. In this sense, a character is someone who is in some way out of step with his or her surroundings. Shakespearean clowns are by definition almost always on the edge of the values of their theatrical world, which enables them to skirt the line between respectability and blasphemy. In *King Lear*, the Fool can say things to the King that no other character can get away with saying, simply because the King sees him as "a character," one who amuses by violating society's rules of propriety.

By tracing character development backward, you can find the arc of each character and get a sense of how the events of the play affect him or her. If you come into rehearsal with a good sense of the major arc of the characters (at least as a starting point for exploration with the actors), it will help you understand and cast the play. If you then cast actors who share your vision of the characters' arcs, the collaboration is more likely to succeed, and the chances that the production will reach its goals improve greatly.

Key character changes reveal themselves more easily in reverse because we gain 20/20 hindsight as play readers. Quite simply, a well-written play should reveal itself to the audience slowly, through a series of surprises and discoveries. By the end of the play, even of the most ambiguous avant-garde play, some of the action and character traits will have become clearer. By focusing first on the clarity or closure provided by the climax and ending, the director and the ensemble gain a better sense of how to read the actions and the characters along the way. For the key moment or key character revelation to stand out, it must build to this final moment of clarity, so that the moment uncovers something that is new and yet linked to previous events. Knowing where a play or scene ends or climaxes provides valuable information about what you should build on throughout the play. From this, you can chart a course, define and shape the action and characters along this route, and lead to a key moment that is surprising, spectacular, or quietly discomfiting.

Number of characters. Examining a play for the number of characters on stage in any scene also reveals a lot to the director about the action of the play. To use a famous example, *Hamlet* ends with a good many dead characters on stage who have killed each other, including the queen, her son, and her new husband/king. Several others have died previously, including Polonius and his daughter, Ophelia. The murder of Hamlet's father sparked much of this action, and it's not hard to see that an element of revenge fuels the action of the play. Conversely, *Twelfth Night*, like many traditional comedies, ends with several couples married or betrothed, and amid the celebrations Malvolio has become the laughingstock of the entire community. What sequence of events brought about all these couplings and pushed Malvolio from his position as Olivia's most respected servant to a near-outcast fool? *The New Rules* ends with one character holding a dead man in his arms. What killed the man? How did the action lead us to that moment? What is the most interesting or compelling way a director can shape the events that lead to this tableau? These questions go to the heart of the director's art and serve as the springboard for the director's creativity in shaping the action.

Environment and number of settings. In plays with multiple settings, the change of setting from one scene to another shapes the action and tells the director a great deal about the play. Look for patterns in settings. Which scenes are indoors versus outdoors? Public versus private? On whose turf do certain scenes occur? What, in your imagination, propels the play from one place to another? A strong choice of theatrical setting should take into account all that the playwright has provided. It might not be the core of the production, but it should work with characters and actions to help shape the core action. In this way, setting is a part of the core action, not a substitute for it. Should you go on to direct productions with designers, expressing your interpretation of the play in terms of core action will allow them the freedom to find their own visualization of the core and bring the full range of their design skills to bear on the production.

Every play gives the director a wealth of information about the world within which it occurs, even those avant-garde plays that avoid specific details about the time, date, and place. In fact, a play set in a no-man's land, such as *The New Rules*, tells you as much about the environment of the play as a detailed, realistic play. The absence of specific, realistic information is as essential to understanding the environment of the play as its presence. In contemporary theater, specifics about setting, particularly in a play that has been produced previously and does not have the playwright in residence, are a director's choice. Some directors prefer to stay close to the playwright's stated intentions about setting; on the other end of the spectrum, some directors diverge greatly from the original setting of the script. As a director, you will find your own approach, which can vary depending upon the particulars of each production.

Frequently, the stage directions in a script reflect the choices that the director and designers made in the first professional production. Often, we cannot be absolutely certain whether the stage directions reflect the playwright's intent, the first director's staging, or the revisions of the first editor to publish the play. If you accept the stage directions as gospel, you severely limit your choices in interpreting the script. Ultimately, it might be impossible to uncover definitively the stated or implied "playwright's intent" unless the director has the playwright in residence.

What, then, can you examine to decide how to position your production in the continuum between strict adherence to the descriptions in the text and complete freedom from them? The text itself is your most concrete guide—not the playwright's intent, but the actual words of the text. What does the text say about the environment? To direct a production that bears a constructive relationship to the text, look closely at the environment—the world of the play—analyzing not only what characters and stage directions tell us about the world, but also what the characters' actions and reactions imply. Part of your job will be to create your version of this world on stage. Whether you choose to stay close to what the playwright calls for in the stage directions or decide to substitute a different setting, be it specific or abstract, you must at the very least recognize and understand the information the playwright provides in the text. You may choose to depart greatly from what the playwright explicitly describes, but you should first understand it, so your decision will be an informed one.

Sound. Over the past couple of decades, sound has become an increasingly essential element of theatrical production. In part, this represents theater's reaction to the successful (and sometimes constant) use of underscoring and environmental sound in film. Technological advances, in particular the ability to manufacture sound and create high-quality recordings inexpensively in various digital formats, have made sound available even for low-budget productions. In fact, if we look at the cost, both in terms of labor and materials, of the four major design areas—sets, costumes, lights, and sound—sound is the least expensive element for a director to incorporate and can produce the greatest "bang for the buck." We'll be looking at how to shape productions with sound later, but for now let's focus briefly on reading a script for ideas about sound.

A director can analyze a script by charting out the explicit or implicit sounds. The director or sound designer might eventually supplement these sounds in production, but what sounds are required? What sounds are suggested, either by the action of the play, the setting, or the dialogue? What sounds might be added as environmental sound or underscoring? In *The New Rules*, what did you find in the way of explicit or implied sounds? Why are these important, and what could you do with them? How is sound significantly tied to the action of the play? Look at the world of the play—which we might describe as a sterile test environment—and the creatures outside that world: the rats that appear to be in charge of the men. Imagine what sounds might underscore or punctuate the action. Where does the playwright want the environment to intrude on the characters? How can sound help to do this?

KEY TERMS

Story.   All the information a play provides about the events that occur on and off stage. Story is chronological and includes all events before, during, and after the action of a play.

Plot. The playwright's selection and ordering of events from the story that occur on stage. Plot need not be chronological; by its nature, it includes only a portion of the complete chronological story.

Core action. The director's choice of the central elements, within or inspired by the text, that will fuel a particular production of a play. The core action should be based on an understanding of the text, but it can emphasize whatever elements the director finds central to his or her interpretation. It will vary from director to director, depending upon the director's ideas, the production space, the cast, and the community for which the play is being produced.

SUPPLEMENTAL READING

Aristotle. *Poetics.* Translated by Gerald F. Else. Ann Arbor: University of Michigan Press, 1967.
David Ball. *Backwards and Forwards: A Technical Manual for Reading Plays.* Reprint, Carbondale: Southern Illinois University Press, 1998.

3 Collaboration in Rehearsal

In ideal production situations, most directors start to prepare to direct a play months before design meetings, auditions, and rehearsals. The director's preparation might include dramaturgical research on the writing of the play, the playwright's other works, accounts of past productions of the play, comparison of translations, and criticism of the play and its genre, as well as background research on any aspect of the world of the play. The director breaks down the script into rehearsal units and analyzes the action, characters, and dramatic structure. This is commonly thought of as the more intellectual (and some would say less creative) side of directing, yet such research and analysis serve as the foundation for a director's creative thoughts, a prelude to the collaboration with the ensemble. As you prepare to work with your ensemble, your research and analysis should help you feel more secure with the fluid interaction of collaboration and better able to make choices from among the options that arise through the work. Preparation, then, is inseparable from collaboration, even though it frequently occurs in the solitude of libraries, studies, and cafés.

One of the risks in learning to direct by first completing a script analysis on paper is that you might start to see the analytical side of directing as detached from what happens in the rehearsal and design process. Script analysis is part of the director's process. It prepares the director for the next step—the rehearsal and design process—but it is not a substitute for the essential collaborative work of the director with his or her ensemble. Although you will analyze the scenes and plays you will work on throughout this book, your analysis must complement the collaboration, rather than rule it. Your understanding of a play should help you lead the ensemble within the collaboration, but it shouldn't lead you to predetermine the results of the process.

Some directors see the rehearsal and design process as a way of achieving a vision they have completed in their minds. This risks creating a strongly hierarchical production system, in which the director makes the vast majority of choices and the ensemble merely does its best to fulfill them. But script analysis is worth the risk because it prepares the director to collaborate. The entire ensemble should analyze the script, using its own tools and focusing on its own areas and ideas. The more prepared the ensemble is going into rehearsal, the stronger the rehearsal collaboration can be. The director should not fall into the trap of rigidly holding to the conclusions drawn from his or her initial analysis, nor should he or she begin rehearsal with little or no preparation. With over-preparation, the director might become inflexible, but with underpreparation, the director will not have a foundation, based on the script, from which to collaborate. The ideal, then, is for you to be thoroughly prepared but flexible.

Aim to enter rehearsal with sufficient depth of understanding of the play to lead. Allow the confidence that comes from familiarity with the play to carry over into your collaboration and make you a more generous collaborator. In this way, your preparation will allow you to evaluate your own choices and those of your collaborators honestly. Script analysis poses a risk to collaboration only when you hold rigidly to your initial ideas or the ensemble members do not meet the challenge of collaboration with their analyses. All theater artists should be thinking artists, able to come to each rehearsal armed with new ideas, open to each other's ideas and new choices that arise from the collaboration.

Directing it is just finding where the winds are and then positioning yourself to say, "Well, I think we should go there." You don't decide where the wind blows, you just try to find out where it is calling.

—Robert Lepage, "Collaboration, Translation, Interpretation" (interview by Christie Carson), *New Theatre Quarterly* 9.33 (February 1993): 31–32.

The question remains: How do we learn to collaborate as theater artists? Rather than start by directing a short scene from a play with a cast of actors from outside the class, you will work in teams of two or three on five- to ten-minute scenes from a full-length play, Harold Pinter's *Betrayal*. Although you may work on a different play, I will refer to *Betrayal* throughout this book for examples, and I suggest strongly that you read the play before proceeding to the next chapter. You will act in the scenes and direct one another, thereby compelling each of you to collaborate on an interpretation; thus, you will each be codirector and actor in your scene. The goal is not simply to create the best final product, but to negotiate and collaborate with one another while staying true to your individual overall interpretation. Together, search for solutions that are stronger than your original ideas for the scene. In beginning your work with actors you already know (your classmates), it should be easier for you to try out new techniques without undue fear of failure. After you and your classmates direct one another as equal collaborators, you will direct cast members from outside the class in a ten- to twenty-minute one-act play.

Your class may read *Betrayal* and limit its use to illustrative examples and exercises in class or use it for the beginning scene work. Should your group require more scenes for women, Pinter's *Old Times*, with two-women and one man, has several two-woman scenes that you might find useful, or you might add scenes from Pinter's other plays or plays by other writers. By using scenes written by the same playwright (and, ideally, from the same play), the class can share its dramaturgical research; this, together with seeing one another's work on a variety of scenes from the play, will add depth to your understanding of the play as a whole. If you prefer to work on a more realistic, contemporary American play, you might consider using scenes from any of the following plays, each of which has several strong scenes for young directors:

Edward Albee, *Three Tall Women* and *The Zoo Story*
Jon Robin Baitz, *The Film Society* and *Substance of Fire*
Rebecca Gilman, *Boy Gets Girl* and *Spinning into Butter*
Richard Greenberg, *Eastern Standard* and *Life Under Water*
Kenneth Lonnergan, *This Is My Youth* and *Lobby Hero*
Craig Lucas, *Blue Window* and *Reckless*
Arthur Miller, *A View from the Bridge* and *The Ride Down Mt. Morgan*
Sam Shephard, *True West* and *Fool for Love*
Paula Vogel, *How I Learned to Drive* and *And Baby Makes Seven*
August Wilson, *The Piano Lesson* and *Ma Rainey's Black Bottom*
Lanford Wilson, *Burn This* and *Redwood Curtain*

In these first scenes, each student should write a preliminary analysis of the scene before rehearsals start; the analysis will be revised and completed as you acquire other directing skills (see Script Analysis and Dramaturgy Checklist at the end of Chapter 4). By starting to write a preliminary analysis before the rehearsal period, you will be able to track how your preliminary ideas changed from preparation to final product. You should write a final analysis of the scene at the end of the process, discussing the process and how the interpretation of the core action changed through collaboration. To monitor the collaborative process and provide feedback to the class, throughout the rehearsal process, you should also make *rehearsal observations*, both in and out of class (see the section on rehearsal observations later in this chapter). I have included a rehearsal feedback form in Appendix A.

If you follow the scheme of this book, each of you will direct a ten- to twenty-minute one-act play (see Appendix C for a listing of one-act plays). One-act plays are complete plays; they might be short, but they contain most of the elements of a full-length play, in condensed form. Most important, short one-act plays display self-contained arcs that directors can shape, and each play will have its own climactic key moment. As such, these plays will provide you with an opportunity to use all your acquired skills on one production. Scene cuttings from full-length plays, though they have the advantage of providing directors with the entire play as background for their work on the piece, are always somewhat jarring when seen out of context. Furthermore, student actors are more likely to audition for one-act plays than scenes, and if you cast from a large pool of actors, you are likely to learn more and your cast is more likely to be of high quality. Last, a director can list a one-act play as a credit on his or her resume. By building your resume at this early stage in your career, you develop credentials and establish experience.

You should cast the plays at one time, bargaining for actors, and your productions can be performed on a single night or on successive weeks as part of a one-act festival (two or three plays on the bill each week) staged throughout campus. Such productions can help to raise the level of awareness and visibility of theater on your campus and bring theater directly into your community. Your resources will be strictly limited so that the project is **poor theater**—a strong foundation for most early directing work. In his theater manifesto *Towards a Poor Theatre* (1968), the Polish experimental theater director Jerzy Grotowski coined the term "poor theatre" to convey the idea of a theatre that depended on the creativity and virtuosity of the ensemble rather than on lavish sets and technical effects. Grotowski argued that theater should be created by focusing on its essence: "The acceptance of poverty in theatre, stripped of all that is not essential to it, revealed to us not only the backbone of the medium, but also the riches which lie in the very nature of the art-form."[1] He embarked on a series of theatrical experiments intended to create theater through the collective work of an ensemble of actors who shared a rigorous physical training regime, performed with only functional costumes, no makeup, and limited lighting and sets, and gave up the proscenium stage for unique performance environments in which actors and audience could interact freely.

But in a more general sense, poor theater has a long and rich history, going back to the earliest Greek theater and the Elizabethan public theaters of Shakespeare's time (see Chapter 5 for more on poor theater). One "dirty little secret" of contemporary professional theater is that your first productions will more closely resemble these poor theater productions than the main-stage productions your college or university produces. Get used to doing everything yourself; early professional theater careers are made from how you respond to what you don't have. Try to find the way to do the impossible with the least resources, and then when you have more, you will use it more efficiently. Figure 3.1 shows an example from a one-man show, and Figure 3.2 illustrates a poor theater production.

The First Scene Collaboration

Directing yourself and your partner in a scene will be difficult and challenging, even if you are fortunate enough to be working with someone you respect and with whom you share an aesthetic. You will encounter questions that are inherent in any directing process but which will be brought to the forefront in this assignment. Who's in charge? How hard should I fight for what I see in the play?

[1]Jerzy Grotowski, *Towards a Poor Theatre* (New York: Simon and Schuster, 1968), p. 21.

FIGURE 3.1 *Sidekick* **by Keith Curran.** Theatre North Collaborative, NYC. A one-person show about a siamese twin learning to walk alone after being surgically detached from his dead brother. The play called for the character to undergo physical therapy on parallel bars, but this inexpensive facsimile focused attention on actor Clark Middleton's virtuosic use of his body.

What's important enough to fight for, and what isn't? When is the working relationship more important than the idea I have for a moment in the scene? Face these issues; discuss them with your partner; bring in a classmate to observe your rehearsal interactions; and bring these issues to the attention of your class at an

FIGURE 3.2 *I Think It Would Be Correct to Do It This Way.* Directed and adapted by Erica Gould from texts by the Italian Futurists. John Slade Ely House, Yale University. The adaptation, design elements, and movement for this production were created through the collaboration of the director and actors during the rehearsals of this "poor theater" production. Photographer: Michael Marsland.

early stage, when differences still can become opportunities for learning, rather than obstacles. Remember that the aim is an extended exploration of how to direct, more than the production itself. Rather than seek to get your way all the time, focus on collaborating effectively with your partner toward a shared final product. As always, describe the issues of your collaboration with sensitivity to the feelings of those involved. Your partner, presumably, will be as fully invested in this assignment as you are, and your success is inextricably tied together. Be diplomatic and respectful but confront the issues. Conflicts will not disappear and should not be brushed under the rug. Collaborators have a duty to one another to voice their concerns early; complaints voiced after the production serve only to exacerbate tensions and hurt the chances of future collaborative work. How you handle conflict and differences of opinion affects your reputation as a collaborator, and you're aiming to build trust and gain a reputation for honesty.

Many of you might find it difficult to direct your own performances; after all, how can you see what you've done? You can't watch your staging; you can only experience it. Through this extended directing exercise, however, you will gather firsthand experience about how to direct as a collaborator, and you will do so in a relatively "safe" environment, with a student who shares your goals. You will see the effects of other directors' efforts, so when you observe the other scenes in your class, you will learn both by doing this work and by seeing the process and results of others. Think of this assignment as an opportunity to experience directing and collaborating, rather than one in which you are under pressure to produce the best product at all costs. Focus on process, not product; stimulate your partner to do his or her best work. By shifting the focus from your acting work to that of your partner, you will have made the first leap toward being a good director, for most successful directors welcome the challenge of facilitating other people's work.

Early on, you might experience one of the primary challenges for any director: a deeply held difference of opinion. How you handle differences of opinion will have a major impact on the rehearsal environment, the success of your process and product, and upon people's perception of you as a director. In future projects, if you reject opinions that appear to conflict with yours, you will find quickly that your cast members will cease to offer opinions and look to you for all direction, or they will resent your imposition of authority. If you seek to placate your cast members by listening to them only as a prelude to rejecting their ideas, you risk being seen as a collaborator in name only: an authoritarian who likes to be thought of as a collaborator. Instead, you should try out your collaborators' ideas whenever time and your interpretation of the play—your core action—permit. If the idea could work within your interpretation and you have time to try it, do so.

There are several reasons for trying out your collaborators' ideas. By doing so, you establish an environment that encourages experimentation even if the ideas ultimately might not be used. And exploring an idea only to discover that it doesn't work often tells you as much about the play or scene as finding a good working solution. A director should be like a scientist, testing out different hypothetical solutions to the problem of producing a play. You aim to get the right answer and hope to minimize the time spent dwelling on avenues of inquiry that are futile, but you accept missteps as part of the path to the ultimate answer.

Again, encourage your ensemble members to feel that they can trust you and one another enough to propose the unthinkable, the outrageous, and the off-kilter; creating an environment in which everyone can do this maximizes the ensemble's ability to create. If the ensemble is afraid to be "wrong," then the production will be safe, and safe productions limit their possibilities for success and learning, both in rehearsal and production. Given the energy it takes to produce a play, a safe production hardly seems worth the effort, particularly if the director does not have a huge budget that he or she needs to earn back in ticket receipts. As budgets increase, risk taking tends to decrease; this is evident in the increasing conservatism of Broadway and Off-Broadway theater in New York. Because you will have small budgets for your first projects, push yourself to take risks and to encourage your collaborators to do the same.

When your ideas about the scene differ from your collaborators', embrace the differences. If you disagree with an ensemble member, try out both ideas whenever possible, unless time or the logic of the core action force you to make a choice immediately. Once two ideas have been tried, the stronger choice should become evident to most, if not all, of the ensemble; if not, let your core action be your guide, and convince your ensemble members that the choice you have tried and selected—be it your original choice or one that a collaborator proposed—works better for the production as a whole. Usually, if you allow everyone to try his or her ideas, you will dispel any residual bad feelings and consequently encourage commitment to the final choice and devotion to continued creative exploration.

Finally, always ask yourself whether the choice is central to your core action. If you differ with an actor, designer, or playwright about a small detail that will not affect the overall interpretation or the shape of the action, it might not be worth winning the argument. The goodwill generated by accepting the suggestion is much more valuable to the final product than the artistic impact of the detail. As a director, you cannot afford to be shortsighted. Keep your eye on the big picture of the production and the process, and keep your ego out of minor decisions as much as possible.

Preparation

Once you embark upon directing as a collaborator, you commit always to justifying your interpretation and to being able to explain it to your ensemble. This places a heavy burden on your preparation, you must be ready to judge all options.

In the next chapter, you will begin to acquire research and analytical skills as you learn how to shape action on stage. First, however, let us see how you will use research in codirecting your first scene. As you begin to work through the exercises in the following chapter, apply analytical skills to your scene as you acquire them. If your entire class is working on one play, then you will be gathering dramaturgical background materials for that play as a group. Start a loose-leaf binder for your scene and add materials about the play, notes, and a working copy of your scene to the binder as you progress. This will serve as an abbreviated form of the total research you would do if you were to direct a production of the entire play.

At the same time, you should begin to go into greater detail on the scene that you are working on with your partner. But—as strange as this sounds—do not read over the scene or discuss it with your partner until you begin rehearsal. Instead, prepare the scene, as a director, for two or three weeks before starting rehearsal with your collaborator. As much as possible, try to use your research and analysis to arrive at an interpretation of your scene that connects with an overall interpretation of the play. Your partner should be equally prepared, so your collaboration will be between two equals—two directors, each with a separate interpretation, who must arrive at and act in an agreed-upon third interpretation. Together you will have generated more ideas about the scene and the play, which should give your process more complex dynamics and more choices from which to select. The final interpretation might be closer to one of your individual interpretations, or it might take a completely new slant on the scene and the play; either way, it should be the result of the give-and-take of two fully prepared theater artists. And you will have to decide when to hold on to your ideas by convincing your partner, and when to be convinced by his or her equal or superior idea. You will have to decide what is important enough to fight for, and what you can concede. In other words, you will have to make collaborative choices toward a mutually agreeable end.

Once you have prepared the scene for rehearsal, you may begin your rehearsal process. This book will sketch a six-meeting schedule for working on the scenes, but you may adapt this model to your course or schedule. Each set of partners should meet the same number of times for the same amount of time. This creates a level playing field upon which to evaluate your work; no one in your class will be able to gain an advantage simply by rehearsing more often. This might seem to limit the initiative of students who wish to work harder, yet the more ambitious student can still spend as much time out of rehearsal working individually on analysis and preparation. By following the steps in this book, you will gain an appreciation of the time pressure that weighs upon almost any directing job and collaboration. In an ideal world, you might have the freedom to try every idea that occurs to you and your partner before arriving at a final interpretation; in the real world, you will probably never have this luxury. The pressure of a time limit helps focus you and your partner on what is most important in the scene, and within these constraints, keeping a positive collaborative relationship is your number one priority. If both of you fail to commit to your collaboration, your scene will suffer, even if you convince your partner to accept everything you see in the scene. You will win the battle but lose the war.

If you follow this book through a fourteen-week semester, you will have three to four weeks to prepare to codirect the first-scene exercise with your partner and three weeks to work on the scene before a midterm presentation of the scene; within a ten-week trimester, the rehearsal period of the first scene may be compressed. To be fully prepared to direct a short one-act play in the second half of the semester, you should have selected the play and completed your preliminary analysis of it by the middle of the semester, so that you can cast the play and begin rehearsals shortly after completing the midterm presentation (see the course outline in Appendix A). This schedule allows time for each of you to find an initial interpretation of the first-scene collaboration and then collaborate toward a revised, shared interpretation.

Sample Rehearsal Schedule

(Two to three hours per rehearsal, over two to three weeks)

> Rehearsal 1: **First read-through** and discussion of **core action** as it relates to the scene and the play. Discuss **character analyses.**
>
> Rehearsal 2: Break down the play into **rehearsal units** and discuss **overall action-objectives.** Discuss and agree upon the **groundplan.**
>
> Rehearsal 3: **Preliminary blocking** and discussion of **unit-by-unit action-objectives.**
>
> Rehearsal 4: **Off-book.** The first rehearsal with actors trying to remember their lines can be frustrating, since it might seem like much of your work has disappeared. Be patient and it will return.
>
> Rehearsal 5: Discuss the **overall arc** of the scene and how it is served by the unit actions. **Fine tuning** of units that seem to detract from the arc.
>
> Rehearsal 6: **Run-throughs** and minor **touch-up** notes and discussions.

Rehearsal Observations

Rehearsal observations can be used to give direct feedback on the way in which directors interact as collaborators: how they explain concepts, handle disagreements, move through the rehearsal space, or deal with any of the other concepts you will be working with in the upcoming chapters. I advocate three types of rehearsal observations:

1. **In-class observations,** in which the entire class watches a director, or a pair of codirectors, at work. The goal of these observations is to share the directing teams' work, challenges, and methods with one another, and to bring the instructor's expertise into the process.

2. **Instructor observations,** in which the instructor attends part or all of a rehearsal outside of class. This type of observation allows the directing teams to interact a bit more naturally, since they will not feel the pressure to perform or behave a particular way, as they might in front of their peers. It can also allow time for more detailed feedback and a more private setting for discussing more ingrained rehearsal problems.

3. **Peer observations,** in which students attend one another's rehearsals. On the surface, peer observations might seem to be the most problematic, since it is difficult to criticize one's peers effectively without hurting their feelings. Yet this is perhaps the most important part of the rehearsal observation, for you will learn almost as much by watching your peers direct as by directing yourself. Moreover, peer observations will help you become a better collaborator, for the process provides another opportunity to collaborate, this time essentially as a production dramaturg. These observations should be written, with copies for the directors and the instructor, and/or discussed during class.

Some ground rules for observations will help keep the process productive:

1. The primary focus of a peer watching a rehearsal should be on **observation.** This should guide peer feedback in class, as well as in outside rehearsal observations. When you attend a peer's rehearsal, your primary responsibility is to tell the director or codirectors what you see. Refrain from directing the scene yourself or giving acting notes. Concentrate on describing to the director what you notice about his or her interactions with collaborators. Refrain from evaluating the product and from passing judgment on the process.

2. Keep in mind that your observations about your peer reflect your **personal point of view.** State your opinion in terms of personal opinion and observation, whether you give a written or an oral observation. Avoid judgmental statements such as, "Your rejection of your actor's idea for the blocking in this scene alienated him or her," in favor of statements that acknowledge your point of view, such as, "I noticed that you didn't try your actor's idea about blocking, and after that, the actor didn't seem as open to your ideas."

3. **Be specific.** General comments about the rehearsal mood are less valuable than specific comments about behaviors. Describe what you see in detail, as if you are capturing it on film. Rather than voicing strong opinions about what works or what doesn't work, describe the rehearsal in enough detail for the director to understand what you saw and then be able to judge whether this achieved his or her aims. Ultimately, each of you must decide whether the rehearsal achieved your personal goals; the observation should help you understand what happened in rehearsal from a more objective point of view. It serves as a "reality check" of sorts, in that it allows you to

see yourself in rehearsal through another person's eyes. The key for the observer is to be as objective and nonjudgmental as possible.

4. **Be constructive.** Although you might not feel comfortable offering advice or alternative solutions to rehearsal problems, you should always keep your comments upbeat and supportive. Even if the work or the process is badly flawed, start from the assumption that your peers are investing themselves fully in their work, and treat them with the respect that you would desire under similar circumstances. You never know when they will be critiquing you or collaborating with you. For this reason, peer teams should evaluate each other's one-acts, so that your comments will always be tempered by the knowledge that you will be receiving comments from the same person you are observing. This does not guarantee that the observations will be smooth and productive. You might be afraid to be completely honest in this situation; others might retaliate for what they viewed as an unnecessarily negative observation. But this, too, is a collaborative situation, so you will learn about constructive collaboration from the act of relating your observations.

Videotaping Rehearsals

Few directing teachers use videotape in the classroom, and until recently I didn't. The reason usually given for abstaining from videotaping rehearsals will be evident to anyone who has seen a videotape of theater: regardless of technological advances, videotape almost always distorts and impairs live performance. We create theater to be seen live, not to be preserved and seen on another medium. Experienced film and television actors know how to alter their acting techniques and the size of their performances for the camera, and film and television employ sound equipment that is vastly superior to what most theater departments will have at their disposal. Still, the instructor can use a video camera to record the students' directing *process*, literally turning the camera on the director instead of the actors, so the instructor and students can see how they collaborate.

SUPPLEMENTAL READING

Bly, Mark, Shelby Jiggets, Jim Lewis, Paul Walsh, and Christopher Baker. *The Production Notebooks: Theatre in Process.* New York: Theatre Communications Group, 1996.
Cardullo, Bert. *What Is Dramaturgy?* New York: Peter Lang Publishing, 2000.
Hodge, Francis. *Play Directing: Analysis, Communication and Style.* Rev. ed. Englewood Cliffs, NJ: Prentice-Hall, 1982.

CHAPTER

4

Directing Elements

A director may have a good sense of what drives a play—what we've been calling the core action—but unless he or she can translate it onto the stage in a compelling way, the interpretation may add little to the power of the words and may in fact detract from it. I use the phrase **directing elements** to refer to fundamental building blocks that help directors achieve their interpretations. Directing elements shape the pattern of a play in production in the same way that a piece of music is shaped by the tones, notes, rhythms, melodies, harmonies, and conductor's choices, or a painting is shaped by the painter's use of size, shape, color, patterns, and the relationships among these.

Almost every script contains textual elements that offer clues to the staging possibilities of the play: components comprised or suggested by the playwright's text, which the director must find and which can serve as a springboard for several possible interpretations of the play. These elements include the structure of the play (such as units, subunits, and key moments); actions and objectives of the characters and the play (moment to moment, scene to scene, and over the course of the entire play); each character's unique, distinguishing qualities; the groundplan (suggested by the setting of the action, but created by the set designer with the director); the frequently shifting relationships among characters; and the language of the play. I find it constructive to see these elements as part of the immense collaboration that goes into staging a play, more akin to clues from the playwright than blueprints. The words themselves may be unchangeable—that is a decision for the playwright and director, controlled by a living playwright's flexibility or a dead playwright's estate[1]—but the director ultimately interprets the play and brings it to life on stage with the ensemble. Through the work of the ensemble, the words take on a more concrete form, one that is embodied on stage and then eventually finds its final form in the minds of the individual audience members. The director uses textual elements as one way of understanding and shaping the action of the play into tangible form on stage.

At the same time, every production employs visceral elements, such as rhythm and tempo, sound and mood, visual composition, movement and gesture,

---

[1]When a playwright dies, the copyright to his or her plays descends to the playwright's estate, controlled by his or her heirs. Some estates guard these rights vigilantly; others are more generous.

environment, and style. These are the living elements of theater, encompassing all that the audience sees and hears on stage. These elements exist uniquely in each production of a play and may differ greatly depending upon the director's interpretation, as well as the contributions and influence of the ensemble, the audience, and the time and place of production. The playwright may describe or imply visceral elements through the text; indeed, some playwrights include extensive stage directions describing the appearance of production elements in precise detail (see, for example, the stage directions in a realistic play by Henrik Ibsen, Arthur Miller, or Tennessee Williams). Yet ultimately visceral elements remain the responsibility of the director in collaboration with the ensemble. Visceral elements can be consolidated under the terms Aristotle used to describe the fourth, fifth, and sixth parts of tragedy, most broadly defined: language (both content and delivery), music, and spectacle. Aristotle considered these to be the least important parts of a good tragedy for a variety of historical reasons—for example, his *Poetics* focuses more on texts than on productions—but the director realizes his or her interpretation of the script by integrating visceral elements and textual elements. Visceral elements define the external shape of the drama: how it looks and sounds; how the action moves; how the world is represented; and how the characters appear to fit within that world.

Together, the textual and visceral elements of directing form the vast majority of the director's tools—what a director and ensemble use to bring a play to life on stage. As you proceed to direct scenes and then longer plays, these tools will help you discover and achieve a shape for the action. You can acquire further hands-on experience with these tools during your work on scenes and plays. You will not have the full range of tools at your disposal at first, nor should you try to employ them all at once. Instead, attempt to master each tool as you explore it and make the most of what you've acquired. You may focus primarily on the textual or visceral first, or you may integrate the two as you explore them. Either way, I recommend that you learn by experience, exploring the use of directing elements through exercises first and then applying them to your scenes in rehearsal. By the time you are ready to direct a complete play, you should have tried out most of the tools under less-pressured circumstances. By acquiring directing skills under workshop conditions, you will feel more confident when you enter rehearsal.

The format for learning about each directing element is similar: an introduction to the directing element, followed by exercises and discussion, and then a summary of ideas you should have discovered or a list of key terms that directors use to describe them. This format is meant to encourage you to experience the concepts first or attempt to solve a directing problem; the summaries then solidify your knowledge, fill in gaps, and provide you with the accepted language for the central ideas. This is a more active way of learning about directing, as opposed to being led through a series of demonstrations, as more traditional textbooks would have you do. If time allows, repeat the exercises after you've read the summary or later in the semester. Because the exercises are experimental, you should find that your solutions will differ from time to time, depending upon your partner, the material, and, one hopes, your growth as a director.

Textual Elements

Structure

When we're talking about plays, what do we mean by "structure"? We will be using the term "structure" rather than "dramatic structure" to focus our attention on the idea of a structural unit, or a set of building blocks if you prefer, rather than on what is "dramatic." In many plays (particularly realistic plays), dramatic structure and structure will be essentially the same: the units of text and action that the director sees as the major units of the play. Yet for some plays (avant-garde plays, for example), the action might at times appear indirect or obscure, and therefore the plays might seem to lack the elements that are traditionally considered dramatic. What can give these plays a shape, then, may have more to do with music, movement, bodies, or various forms of repetition. Absent traditional dramatic structure, what might we find in the text to suggest a shape or structure for what will be seen on stage? Can we, in some larger sense, define structure so that it will be useful for analyzing and staging any play?

When we examine a play for its structure, we are looking for the clues suggested by the text, which may lead us to grasp an organizing principle for what happens on stage. Ancient Greek tragedies, for example, usually alternated between scenes among two or three characters and choral interludes. The choral interludes themselves can be divided into *strophe* and *antistrophe*, which many scholars define as movement in one direction and then the other. Whereas the structure of a Greek tragedy may be one of the easiest to detect because it can be seen is such tangible terms (a two- or three-character unit of dialogue followed by a choral unit involving dance and music, and so on), directors usually look toward the structural units of a play for guidance in shaping the action. Playwrights emphasize the structure of their plays in many forms: act or scene breaks, whether in writing or implied (as in Shakespeare, for example); "French scenes," in which character entrances and exits define units (as in many of the plays of Moliére); shifts in the subject matter of the dialogue (most readily apparent in language- or thematically driven plays, such as those of George Bernard Shaw); or major changes in mood, conflict, tempo, or rhythm. These are just some of the ways in which playwrights can indicate or imply structure so that directors may uncover or establish the structure in production.

The basic building blocks of a play's structure are called units. A unit is always smaller than an act. Unless a scene is very brief, as is sometimes the case in Shakespearean and Elizabethan plays, a scene usually contains at least two or three distinct units, in order to give it some shape or form. Breaking down a play into units is a subjective art, though. Even if two directors both intend to be true to a playwright's intentions, they may each select a different set of units, depending upon how they interpret the play. These differences help define the artistic choices of your production. The placement and number of units in a director's breakdown of the script affect the rhythm and tempo of the production. Conversely, a director may select particular units because he or she wishes to emphasize certain moments, conflicts, or relationships in a play. Think of the unit breakdown as a series of interconnected choices on your part. Be sure to examine alternatives to what you may initially see as the units of the play, and think about how each possible unit choice affects the overall interpretation of the play.

When we analyze structure, we look for shifts and patterns, particularly those between units, scenes, and acts. Yet what you see as a minor shift within a single unit, another director might envision as defining the boundaries of the unit; these differences play a large part in defining each director's interpretation and the overall shape of the production. One way of finding shifts between units is to look for movement of some sort: a character coming in or going out, a change in subject matter, or a shift in location. This basic structure can often be seen in an act or scene breakdown chart, as you will see below.

As the director, you have leeway in interpreting the structure of the plays you direct for your production through your choice of units, but start with the text itself and observe what the playwright has given you. How many acts or scenes are there? If the playwright has not delineated the action into acts or scenes, do the entrances and exits of major characters indicate the units? Are there shifts in place or time? What is the organizing principle of the play?

EXERCISES

Divide the class into groups of two. Each person should then examine *Betrayal* or your lab play for its structure; any play that all the students have read will serve our purposes.

1. In ten to twenty minutes, mark the major units of the play (beyond the largest and most obvious act and scene breaks) and describe the basis of this structure. Pass your analysis to your partner and reply to his or her analysis, either agreeing or disagreeing with his or her vision of the structure of the play, or arguing for a compromise or an alternative structure. Continue until you have agreed upon a structural principle and basic units or reached an impasse. Share the results with the class.

2. Consider one particular scene from the play. Again, analyze the structure of the scene and describe the organizing principle. Number each unit and be as precise as possible about the exact moment it begins and ends. Write down your ideas and pass them back and forth to your partner until you have reached agreement, synthesis, or impasse.

3. Using one unit breakdown from the class for a scene from the play, title each unit with a short quote from the unit, no longer than seven words.

Pass your unit titles to your partner and discuss the various possible choices. Concentrate on finding the overall pattern of the units through the progression of quotes. Attempt to arrive at a consensus and then share the results with the class.

Discussion

1. How long does a unit need to be? How many units can a play have? Is there a right or wrong number of units?

2. How did the play structure differ from the scene structure? Did some of you see the same play or scene in structurally different ways? What happens when you do so?

3. How might a different structure affect rehearsal and production? How can a director clarify the structure usefully and creatively?

4. What propels a scene from unit to unit or a play from scene to scene? How can a director help his or her actors bridge the gap between units so that the units become building blocks rather than isolated or disruptive moments? Can you image a play or production in which disruptive units might be used as an organizing principle, or must all productions move fluidly from unit to unit?

Climactic and Episodic Structure

Traditional theater scholars have defined dramatic play structure as falling along a spectrum from climactic to episodic. In *The Theater Experience*, Edwin Wilson distinguishes between climactic and episodic structure by examining seven elements:

1. **Point of attack.** Where does the plot start in relation to the overall story? A plot that starts near the beginning of the story has an early point of attack; one that begins near the end of the story has a late point of attack.
2. **Scenes.** Does the play have a few long scenes or many short scenes?
3. **Places.** Is the play set in many places or just one or a few locations?
4. **Characters.** Does the play have a lot of characters or a few?
5. **Plot.** Is there a single dominant plot or are there parallel plots?
6. **Causality.** Does each important action of the play lead to the next in a linear manner, or do they accumulate without a clear causal thread?
7. **Action.** Is the action compressed or spread out in time?

Climactic plays tend to have more condensed features: a late point of attack; few scenes, places, and characters; a single plot; a linear structure; and compressed action. *Episodic plays* tend to be more sprawling: an early point of attack; many scenes, places, and characters; more than one plot line; actions that accumulate; and an expansive sense of action. Many plays combine elements from each type of dramatic structure. Scholars often categorize many of the full-length plays of Bertolt Brecht, such as *Mother Courage and Her Children* and *Caucasian Chalk Circle*, as episodic or *epic*, a term Brecht redefined to have broader purposes, but which includes episodic structure among its primary features. Single-setting realistic plays, such as Ibsen's *Hedda Gabler*, frequently exemplify climactic structure because of the preponderance of compressed elements. The dichotomy between episodic and climactic structure helps us understand the different ways plays function structurally.

These larger categories can be useful in describing the outermost ranges of the continuum: plays that are dominated by episodic or climactic elements. Yet each structural element or variation helps a director grasp how a play functions in rehearsal and production, regardless of whether you categorize it as predominantly episodic, climactic, or a blend of the two. Each play usually has one or two dominant elements that help drive the play forward and suggest a shape. Emphasizing a particular element might provide the central focus for your interpretation. For example, the structure of *Betrayal* is formed in large part by the way in which it moves backward and forward in time; the climax of its plot comes at the chronological beginning of the story. A director might describe the action of the play as being structured by time, and therefore time may be the great shaping force for one interpretation of the play. Consequently, this would have implications for design choices, stage configuration, blocking, actors' actions and objectives, scene transitions, music—any and all of the visceral and textual elements of the production.

Experiment with some structural elements in the following exercises, and then you may discuss the implications of the elements for whatever play or scene you are working on.

STRUCTURE EXERCISES

1. Make a chart of each scene in *Betrayal* or your lab play. On the top horizontal row, put each character in a separate box. On the left vertical column, put the most basic divisions of the play: acts, scenes, or basic units of action, such as French scenes. Go through the play and put an X for a character's appearance in any particular scene in the corresponding box. If the appearance is brief, invent a notation for this type of appearance: a color code or different type of mark that you will easily be able to read off the chart. Aim to create a visual document that shows the number of appearances of each character, with whom they appear, and how their appearances are distributed throughout the course of the play. For Ibsen's *Hedda Gabler*, if we divide the five acts into French scenes, the chart might look something like Figure 4.1, depending upon where you place the unit breaks.

2. Examine your chart individually and generate a list of three to five observations you can draw from it. Working in teams of two to four, iso-

FIGURE 4.1 Sample scene breakdown for *Hedda Gabler*. The first column on the left lists each act and unit numbers within it. (X) = a brief appearance.

	Aunt Julie	Berta	Tesman	Hedda	Thea	Brack	Løvborg
I,1	X	X					
I,2	X	X	X				
I,3	X		X	X			
I,4		X	X	X			
I,5			X	X	X		
I,6				X	X		
I,7		X	X	X	X	X	
II,1				X		X	
II,2			X	X		X	
II,3		X	X	X		X	
II,4			X	X		X	X
II,5			X	X		X	X
II,6		(X)		X	X		X
II,7				X	X	X	X
II,8		X		X	X		
III,1		X		X	X		
III,2		X	X	X			
III,3		X	X	X		X	
III,4				X	X		X
III,5				X			X
IV,1	X		X	X			
IV,2			X	X			
IV,3			X	X	X		
IV,4			X	X	X	X	
IV,5			X	X	X	X	
IV,6		(X)	X	X	X	X	

late the most powerful or important observations that the majority of the group agrees upon. Compare the observations of the groups within the class. For example, based upon the chart above, I might make the following observations: once Hedda appears on stage, she appears in every unit, whereas Løvborg only appears in Acts Two and Three; and Brack appears on stage with every character except Aunt Julie. Discuss the observations from your play among the class as a whole. What inferences can you draw from the scene breakdown?

3. Working with the same teams, focus on three observations from your charts. Each team may work on the same three observations or on a different set of them. What can you deduce from the information you have observed? For example, Hedda's nearly continuous presence on stage

might lead to any of the following deductions, ranging from the obvious to the more speculative: Hedda is the central character; Hedda is a controlling character; this play occurs in Hedda's world. Discuss the observations among the class as a whole.

4. Examine the observations in combinations, and see if you deduce anything further. For example, I might argue that because Hedda appears in every unit after the first one, that she is the protagonist, but that Løvborg's absence from Acts One and Four makes it unlikely that he is the antagonist. Therefore, looking at the chart again, who is Hedda's antagonist? Your choice would lead to a particular core action for the production, and consequently it might greatly affect your ensemble's choices. If, however, you decide that Hedda's primary conflict is with Løvborg, then Act Three becomes the climactic act. You would then have to figure out the function of Act Four within the overall structure of the play. What does your chart reveal about your play?

Discussion

1. Looking over all of the deductions your class has made about the characters' appearances and combinations on stage, can you isolate one or more dominant structural concepts at work in the play? To what extent do the characters drive the play?

2. Do you detect any patterns to the characters' appearances on stage? What qualities of each character help define the conflict or distinguish them from the other characters?

3. Add scene locations to your chart. Is there a pattern to the locations? How do these shifts relate to the character appearances?

TIME EXERCISES

1. Working individually, make a list of the time at which each scene in *Betrayal* or your lab play occurs. Between each scene on the list, note the passage of time occurring. Whereas *Betrayal* serves as an unusual example of a playwright's use of time, because it alternates between "traditional" movement forward in time and jumps backward in time, starting with scene one in 1977 and ending with scene nine in 1969, all playwrights make choices about the use of time, selecting either long uninterrupted periods of time, or particular gaps between scenes or acts.

2. Compile three lists: (1) events that the script clearly indicates occur between scenes; (2) events the script implies occur between each scene; and (3) events you might infer occur between scenes, based however loosely

on the script. Compare lists with a partner in the class. Put a check mark next to any item on the lists that you each agree is supported by the script. Compare your conclusions with those of the rest of the class. What are the most compelling events the class noticed? How justified are the implied or inferred events? What is the difference among the three lists? Of the events not clearly indicated in the script, which do you believe is justified and how would such offstage action affect a director's interpretation of the script?

3. Examine the first and last scenes of the play. Why does the play begin and end where it does? Draft a one-paragraph statement making a case for the significance of the beginning and ending points of the play. Pass it back and forth with your partner until you reach consensus or impasse.

4. For the next class, bring in either: (a) music that captures the overall passage of time in the play, or (b) music that conveys the passage of time between any two scenes in the play. Find the music first, and then write a one-paragraph statement explaining your choice. How does music describe, suggest, and help define the shape of the action?

Discussion

1. How much of the work in the exercises above is analytical and how much is intuitive? Can intuitive responses capture an analytical angle or view of the action of the play? Or do we more frequently resort to justifying intuitive responses regardless of their merit?

2. Do you believe your tendency is to rely on the intuitive or the analytic? Which do you find produces the best results?

Actions and Objectives

What is an objective? From your previous experiences as an actor or acting student, you have probably arrived at an accepted definition of this term. But actors and directors use the word "objective" in a variety of ways. Stanislavski coined the term at the beginning of the twentieth century, but his various disciples have used it in different ways, and in its translation to American and British English, some variety has crept into the denotations and connotations of this key term. Some of the confusion comes from the companion term "action." The proliferation of terms used as substitutes for objective, such as "need," "want," or "desire," has added to the confusion. Let's clarify what we mean when we use these terms.

For the actor, an **objective** is what his or her character wants, needs, or desires. These terms—objective, action, need, want, desire—are often used interchangeably, although actors and directors differ on the distinction between objective and action, and thus among their synonyms as well. Some actors and directors include the verb and the desired response within the objective. For our purposes, I think it is clearest to state that an action is a verb and an objective is a desired outcome: what the character wants the other character(s) to do. As William Ball puts it, "A superior, more subtle, and certainly more actable expression of the want will include the person to whom the want is directed and the response sought from that person."[2] An action is a verb: what the character will do to the other character(s) to get their objective. I view needs, wants, and desires as synonyms for objectives—outcomes that the character pursues—but it is best to clarify this terminology early in the rehearsal process to minimize confusion among the cast. As you direct more, you will find actors who have learned different variations of Stanislavski's system and therefore use different terminology in different ways. Some actors may resist using the word "objective" because they see it as too analytical. By understanding the synonyms, a director can better adapt to each actor's training and knowledge. Find the language that works best for you and your cast; adapt it to individual actors to maximize your ability to communicate with and among them.

One more term might be useful to introduce: the **super-objective**. Stanislavski coined this term to describe the single driving need, want, or desire of each character over the course of the entire play. He believed each character is motivated primarily by a single objective in the play—the super-objective—that they might pursue through a variety of short-term actions over the course of the play. Each character's super-objective remains consistent throughout the play, but along the way, a character may have different objectives for individual acts, scenes, or units. The super-objective brings all of these smaller or short-term objectives together in some way. In other words, the characters' objectives throughout a play should have something to do with their super-objectives. Frequently, the unit objectives are steps along the way to the super-objective. It is normal, though, for characters to occasionally undercut themselves; a character may therefore pursue a unit or scene objective that runs counter to his or her super-objective. This can add complexity to a production, by allowing the characters to fail to reach their objectives. The changes in how a character pursues his or her super-objective, and the actions and objectives each actor chooses to play within each scene or unit—which will vary depending upon who is in the scene, how much success or failure the character has experienced in attempting to achieve his or her super-objective, and when and where each scene occurs—will suggest a range of character arcs from which each actor will create his or her character's journey. As Michael Shurtleff writes in *Audition*, actors need to be aware of the opposite of their objective, since characters often sabotage their own best efforts.

Actions may be described in various ways. Within the Stanislavski system, and most contemporary versions and derivatives of the system, an **action** is a playable verb: a concrete action that an actor can pursue for several minutes. It

[2]William Ball, *A Sense of Direction* (New York: Drama Book Publishers, 1984), p. 79.

should be an active verb, a word we would use easily in everyday conversation. In his book *A Sense of Direction*, William Ball categorized types of verbs that actors should avoid because they are unplayable: intellectual, behavioral, existential, adjectival, or trigger verbs. Finding a playable verb can be difficult and frustrating for young actors at first. Many actors believe that they understand what the character is doing and fear that specifying a word for this action might limit their ability to play a scene freely. They may prefer to keep this process intuitive. As a director, if you find that a particular scene is working without discussing the actions with the actors, you may wish to trust the scene as is. With experienced professional actors, this often works. But keep in mind that Stanislavski invented the system and terminology of actions to keep his own acting performances from losing their inspiration over the course of repeated performances during the run of a production. By changing the action or verb in any scene, while retaining the objective, he believed he could refresh a scene that had gone stale, reinvigorating it or finding a new path through the scene. For this reason, even if a scene plays very well early in rehearsal, you may wish to reconsider the actors' choices about actions and objectives at a later point if the scene appears to be losing vital energy or clarity.

Discussing actions with actors also allows the director to share the interpretation of a scene with the actors, shape the scene's place within the overall play, and make actors aware of the characters' arcs throughout the play. Difficult scenes can be unlocked through such discussions, and new approaches can be discovered. It might help to tell your actors that they will learn something even from a "wrong" choice. This gives them the latitude to experiment and take chances, free of the fear of failure. Finding a character's actions should be a laboratory exploration among the actors and director. By its nature, this is a collaborative venture. If you give your actors the freedom to try out new actions and objectives, it increases the feeling that the actors own their roles. In most cases, my experience has been that this feeling of ownership outweighs the benefits of directors "getting their way." Particularly on a unit or scene level, different actions may work within the same overall shape of the director's interpretation. Choose your battles. Always ask yourself whether your interpretation of a particular moment is essential to your overall core action. If it is, it's worth fighting for. But more times than not there are several ways to get to the same place, and actors who feel their opinions are respected and their contributions are taken seriously and are used will usually turn in better performances.

William Ball's comprehensive formula for actions and objectives is a useful way to integrate these elements. A character wants to do something (the *action*: a playable verb) to someone (the other character or *receiver*) to get something (the *objective*: a reaction from the other character). Let's look at some playable examples:

Roger wants *to dominate* his business partner *to give up control.*
Jennifer wants *to impress* her boss *to give her a raise.*
Tom wants *to soothe* his wife *to forgive him.*
Mary wants *to interrogate* her roommate *to find out about someone she likes.*

In these examples, the actions—belittle, impress, soothe, interrogate—are everyday things that an actor can do to another actor for a significant period of time. The objectives are to gain control, to get a raise, to obtain forgiveness, to learn about someone. Any major unit will have an overall objective for each character as well as an overall action for the unit. But the most interesting scenes usually involve changes in actions. As a director, you're looking for moments in the text that suggest an actor has changed his or her action. Such moments give the unit shape, suggest a give-and-take between the actors, and help define their relationship. Directors and actors sometimes use the word "tactic" as well. Although many people use tactic and action interchangeably, I find that tactic connotes that the character knows what he or she is doing, whereas an action can be either spontaneous or planned. If you accept this distinction, then a tactic refers to a conscious maneuver on the character's part, and this may tell you something about how conscious the character is of his or her own desires.

A number of things may trigger a change in the action of a character, and directors search for these moments of change in preparing a script and in rehearsing it. As you begin to direct, note these changes in your script. As you gain more experience as a director, you may become comfortable writing down less of your analysis, but it should always be something you recognize and understand in each scene. One of the keys to using this type of script analysis within a collaborative process is your willingness to try out and discuss different moments of change and various actions with your actors. To do so, your actors will need to be able to express themselves in a shared language, whether you use the terms action and objective, or your ensemble settles upon different terminology with which you feel more comfortable. Encourage them to come to rehearsal prepared for these discussions, having written down their own analysis of actions and objectives. The actor/director collaboration improves when everyone is willing to discuss and contribute to decisions. Yet ultimately your position as the director—the leader of the production—gives you authority over the overall choices. By remaining open to your actors' ideas, you establish a more collaborative environment, in which actors feel safe to try out things and to speak up. But you retain the power and the responsibility for making the final choices. In doing so, keep your attention on the big picture: the overall objective and shape of the production. There may be many possible choices that will contribute to the overall shape. Inevitably, your actors will discover a range of choices, some of which may have occurred to you and others that have not. Balance the benefits of a shared creative process with the needs of the overall production. The next exercises will examine how this process of collaborating on actions and objectives can work before we go into greater depth about the shifts and changes in objectives and between actions.

EXERCISES

Using a scene with two characters from *Betrayal* or your lab play, split up into teams of two and analyze what each character's action and objective might be.

1. Each of you should write down what you see as the overall action/objective for each character in the scene on a piece of paper or on a photocopy of the scene. Express the action/objective for each character in terms of the formula suggested above: A wants to do something (an action, a verb) to B (the other character in the scene) to get something (a response of some sort from B). B wants to do something to A to get something.

2. Trade copies of the scene. Discuss the differences in your views without trying to persuade your partner to agree with you. Merely note the differences.

3. Revise your action/objective analysis based on what you see and what you have learned from your partner. One way to test your analysis is to make sure that each character's objective conflicts with one of the others. If they are not in conflict, try to adjust your action or objective to bring out the conflict in the scene.

4. Trade copies of the scene with your partner again. Discuss the strengths of each and try to come to a consensus on an approach to the scene. Share your final decisions with the class.

5. Take two or three of these action/objective analyses and test them on their feet, with students in the class playing the two roles. Discuss the differences among the various approaches. Is there a difference between what works best on the page versus the stage? Are there combinations of actions and objectives still worth exploring? What did you learn from approaches that did not seem to work on stage?

Summary

This is one way for the director to find the shape of a scene, and eventually a play, and build a production. A certain amount of this work must be done on paper by the director prior to casting the play, because the director's casting and work with designers must be based on an overall shape or concept for the production for the director to make casting and design choices that will reflect and enhance the interpretation. Your actors should be able to play a strong action/objective for several minutes, and you should be able to find a way to express the overall intention of any scene to your ensemble in this shared language.

Shifts and Key Moments

Within each scene or unit, however, smaller shifts occur as well. These shifts create shape from moment to moment. Just as a play has a climactic moment—the time when the conflict reaches its height—each scene has a mini-climax or what Michael Shurtleff, in his book *Audition*, calls a "key moment." **Shifts** happen any time a character changes his or her action. A **key moment** occurs when the action in a scene reaches a peak. Shifts and key moments can be subtle; they need not be the moments of greatest speed or volume. In fact, using a variety of volumes and tempos will help accentuate the shape of a scene, though the director and actor control the range of these choices. Some key moments work well performed softly and slowly, and the shifts within the scene occur within a limited range. Others scenes may work quickly and boldly, with conspicuous shifts and key moments. Many scenes can be performed with a combination of small, subtle shifts and larger, more obvious ones. And the same scene can be performed successfully in a variety of ways, tempos, and shapes. Your ensemble should explore these choices in rehearsal, and your decisions will help define your interpretation of the scene or play in production.

EXERCISES

In teams of two, examine a scene that you have already analyzed for action/objective. Working by yourself first, try several approaches to finding the shifts in the scene.

1. First, try looking at the scene intuitively. Read the scene to yourself, and every time you sense a shift in the action of the scene, mark an "S" in a circle next to it. Don't overdo it; mark the major shifts that you see. Compare your notes with those of the class or your partner.

2. Examine the scene again, and look for shifts caused by any of the following:
   - A character changes the *subject*
   - A character appears to change his or her *tactic* or *action*
   - A character provides or discovers *new information*
   - A character *realizes* something for the first time
   - A character makes a significant *physical action*

   Mark these shifts with an "S" in a circle as well, and compare them to your original marks. Compare your analysis to your partner's. Can you agree upon which shifts are the most significant? Share your findings with the class.

3. This time, look for the key moment in the scene. If you have a good sense by now of the conflict that you believe fuels the scene, look for the moment when that conflict either is resolved or reaches a point at which it cannot be resolved. In the alternative, simply look for what appears to be the most important moment in the scene. Mark the key moment with a "K" in a triangle. Can you structure your other choices around this moment? Is the key moment consistent with the focus of the majority of the action of the scene?

4. Evaluate your choices with your partner in writing, passing it back and forth between the two of you. You may argue for your interpretation of the scene, but the objective is to reach the most effective interpretation, regardless of who came up with particular ideas. Share your final analysis of the scene with the class.

Discussion

As you've examined this scene, you've worked from large overall objectives to the small moments that trace the path of actions through the scene. Reverse the analysis in the group discussion. Start by comparing what each team has selected as the key moment.

1. Given the choice of key moment, does the scene have a different focus? What are the strengths and limitations of each choice?

2. Examine the shifts in action along the way, and discuss the significance of each shift. Which are central to the shape of the scene?

3. Do some shifts have greater significance in combination with a particular key moment?

4. Reexamine your team's action/objective for each character. Given what you've decided about the key moment and shifts, would you now choose to revise your actions or objectives?

Summary

Think of shifts as being the most common landmarks within each unit of the play. Shifts map the characters' route through the units in terms of changes in action or tactic. In this way, your reading of where the action shifts occur and what they consist of will help shape the audience's understanding of the characters, the action, and their significance. The characters' action shifts give the play texture in performance. Your collaborative decisions with your ensemble about actions reveal the production's interpretation of what motivates the characters and what they are willing to do to get what they want. Choice of action may also imply tempos and rhythms, or at least suggest a range of possibilities. "To interrogate" or "to soothe" each suggest a different range of possible tempos and rhythms. Thus, these choices shape not only each individual character, but also combine with each other to create a major part of the overall tempo and rhythm of the production, further shaped by design choices.

Key moments, then, are the major landmarks of the play. They map the major turning points—the highs and lows—of the action of the play. You must find the key moments and interpret them consistently with your core action to bring the play to life. To whatever extent possible, try to bring appropriate emphasis to the key moments through all the directing elements at your disposal.

Groundplan

A **groundplan** is a top view of the stage space, drawn to scale, within which the production's action will occur, indicating the exact placement of all walls, stairs, levels, windows, doors, and large properties such as furniture. It is also a tool for communication, both to your actors and your audience, because the way in which the groundplan shapes the space reveals much about the how the director and designers view the possible uses of the space, its owner(s), and its purpose. The groundplan provides you with the opportunity to create a variety of physical relationships among the characters onstage and shapes the possible patterns of movement that the characters might follow during the action. One way to discover how groundplans communicate such information is to examine the spaces you experience in real life as if they were theater spaces. How do the spaces in which you live and work function, and what can you infer from their groundplans? By observing the world in which you live, you will begin to develop some of your own ideas as to how groundplans might influence action, relationships, and character development on stage. Keep in mind that theatrical space does not usually follow the same rules as real space. Once you put an audience at a particular vantage point, for example, the groundplan needs to maximize the sight lines, compositional potential, and blocking possibilities for the particular theater space and stage configuration. For now, let's start by examining the spaces around you.

EXERCISES

1. In small groups, draw a groundplan for two indoor spaces on campus: offices, classrooms, dorm rooms, lounges, cafés, or any other space that your group can recall somewhat accurately. Try to pick two spaces that function differently, even if their overall purpose may be similar. List at least three important features of each groundplan and compare them. From the groundplan, what can you deduce about how the space might be used, what sort of relationships the space encourages, what sort of movement might occur, and what the overall purpose of the space might be?

2. As a class, draw and examine the groundplan for an outdoor space on campus. How does an outdoor space function differently than an indoor space? How does a public space differ from a private space? What is communicated by the outdoor space your class examined? What choices did the original planners of the space make? What choices could they have made instead, and how would the space function and communicate differently given each set of choices?

3. Select one of the spaces above and place it in a real or hypothetical theater. How might the groundplan be best adjusted to suit the theatrical setting and the placement of the audience? What types, genres, or styles of plays might require or suggest different adjustments to the groundplan? How might your decisions about character suggest additional adjustments?

Look at some examples of how an actual indoor space might be adapted for a hypothetical stage. Consider how the office in Figure 4.2 might be rendered on a proscenium stage:

If the drawing below was in ½-inch scale, then every ½ inch of the drawing would represent a foot of an actual stage. The office would be approximately eight feet by ten feet. You can use a scale rule or a regular ruler to measure the dimensions of spaces accurately.

If we remove the downstage wall (the long wall at the bottom of the drawing, with two bookcases and a door), what sorts of blocking and composition issues would the director, set designer, and actors face? What changes can you make to the groundplan to improve it for the proscenium stage? You may notice that a great many "real-life" groundplans lack furniture in the middle of the room. People frequently lay out their rooms this way to increase the amount of open space and make the rooms feel larger. But in many cases on a stage, the actors benefit from having furniture in the middle of the space, with areas in which they can sit spread throughout the stage. This encourages actors to move from area to area, go around large objects, and use the space more actively. Actors will frequently gravitate toward furniture, either to sit or lean on. Furniture, door, and window placement predetermines the possible compositions and movement. A flexible groundplan—one that provides the cast and director with

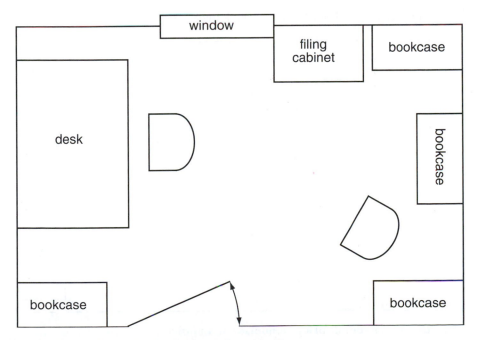

FIGURE 4.2   Scale drawing of hypothetical office.

many different combinations of positions and movements—stimulates the ensemble members to shape their use of the space.

There are several techniques the director and designer can use to create a more flexible and active groundplan. When you direct your first play, you may not have a designer, so you will need to know how to design your own groundplan. Later, when you have the opportunity to work with designers, you will be able to use your knowledge of groundplans to collaborate with your set designer on the most effective groundplan, because you will be able to communicate your concerns from firsthand experience.

FURTHER GROUNDPLAN EXERCISES

1. As individuals, change the dimensions, angles of walls, and placement of objects from one of the previous set of exercises to create your own groundplan. Compare your groundplan with a partner's and then collaborate on a groundplan. What techniques did you discover for converting the real-life office space into a more playable stage space?

   Figure 4.3 shows one possible solution to creating a groundplan for an office on a proscenium stage. While this groundplan is an im-

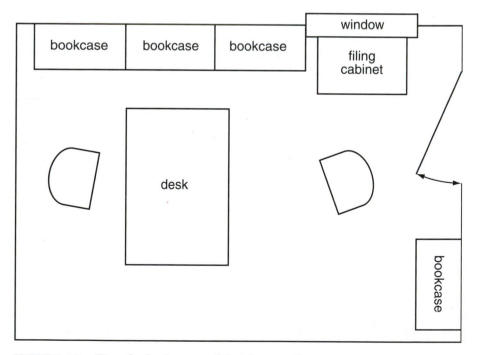

FIGURE 4.3 **First draft of a groundplan for an office.**

provement over the actual office space, it still limits the number of possible compositions and blocking plans; the two seats put characters in profile on the same plane of the stage together, leaving the director no angled compositions; the entrance is largely blocked from view by the downstage left bookcase; and the space is somewhat cramped. It does, however, open up the action to the audience better; suggest that the owner of the desk is in a position of power, due to the central placement of the desk; and clear the downstage area for better viewing through the invisible "fourth wall" that proscenium stages assume as a convention.

Several things can be done to improve the groundplan, based on conventions of the proscenium stage. The conventions of each stage configuration (proscenium, thrust, and arena representing the three major configurations) can help a director greatly. You don't have to follow these conventions or limit yourself to them, but knowing they exist may stimulate you to design your groundplan differently to make it more active and playable. For a proscenuim stage, these conventions include:

- Opening up the stage right and left walls at 30 to 45 degree angles to permit better sight lines for the audience.
- Adding irregular features to the line of the walls, such as an inset corner or a window seat.
- Tilting the orientation of the room toward the audience by 30–45 degrees, so that the orientation of the space is at an angle to the audience.
- Placing furniture, such as chairs, in the downstage right and left corners to give the actors a reason to move to these areas.
- Adding levels or stairs to the groundplan to provide the actors with higher and lower playing areas.

Follow-up Groundplan Exercise

2. Using at least three of the conventions listed above, revise your groundplan to expand its compositional and blocking possibilities. Do not feel constrained by the original dimensions of the space; feel free to add or subtract objects that could be found in an office, such as an extra chair or low bookcases. Discuss the various ways these conventions can be used. What are the changes each of you have made to your original groundplan? Two possible revised groundplans for the office are shown in Figures 4.4 and 4.5. The first one rotates the orientation of the room to the audience, and the second opens up the stage right and left walls.

Summary
Many techniques will help you create more active and playable groundplans. You and your fellow directors may have discovered many of these:

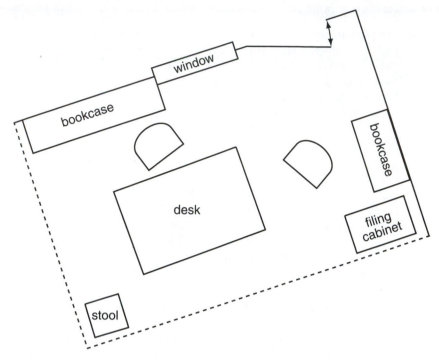

FIGURE 4.4   Groundplan for office with 20 degree counterclockwise rotation.

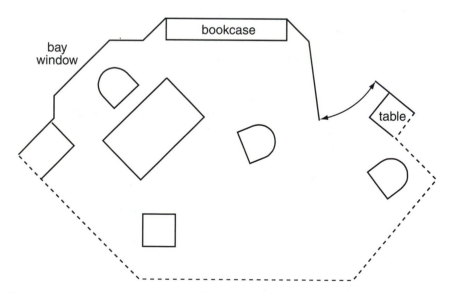

FIGURE 4.5   Groundplan for office with opened-up walls, asymmetry, and some architectural detail.

- Angled compositions
- Angled spaces
- Angled walls
- Asymmetrical spaces
- Architectural details
- Placement of furniture on all planes
- Significant placement of major furniture and doors

Define and discuss your findings, explaining how your groundplans use the concepts above and expanding the list. Test your groundplans by imagining how the characters might move through the space. How many different compositions are possible on the set with both characters sitting or one character sitting and one standing? Are there obstacles—pieces of furniture, like a desk—around which characters can move or confront each other? Will the characters be able to use the entire space? Divide the space into three sections horizontally: upstage, center stage, and downstage. Check to see if all *planes* of the stage can be easily used by the actors. Divide the space vertically as well to make sure that the far right and left sections of the stage will be well utilized. If you design your groundplan on a computer, you can overlay a grid on top of the plan to see how the space is laid out to test whether the groundplan has an overall sense of balance and encourages actors to use all the planes of the stage (see Figure 4.6).

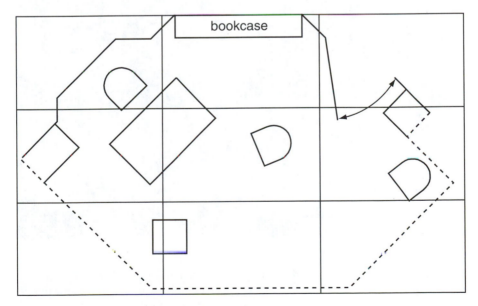

FIGURE 4.6   Groundplan tested on grid.

After examining the groundplan on a grid, what changes might you suggest? Note that the downstage left corner (the bottom right corner of the grid) has nothing in it. What could be added or adjusted to give actors the opportunity to use this part of the space? Are there sufficient obstacles throughout the space to allow for interesting patterns of movement? Which objects receive the most emphasis in the groundplan by virtue of their position? Is the emphasis consistent with the scene you imagine occurring in the space? Are the entrances and windows in significant positions? Does the groundplan offer the director and actors various *levels* for action? Levels can be created by seating and furniture, as well as by platforms. Think in three dimensions: Are there sufficient ways for the actors to use the space so that they are not always eye to eye? Levels allow for disparities in the actors' spatial relationships to each other and may reflect or even contradict the power relationships at work (see Figure 4.7).

Character

What defines a character? At first glance, the list is nearly endless: occupation, age, size, looks, background, class, needs, likes and dislikes, relationships, energy level, sense of humor (or lack thereof). All of these remain open to the interpretation of

FIGURE 4.7 *Tattoo Girl* **by Naomi Iizuka.** Cobalt Theatre Ensemble at the Viaduct, Chicago. Director: Shade Murray. Scene Design: Lynne M. Koscielniak. With a simple platform and ladders, the set provides multiple opportunities for the use of levels.

the actor and director, tempered and steered by the designers, whose choices inform the subsequent choices of the actor. When a costume designer begins to make choices about what each character wears, the collaboration about the character among the costume designer, the actor, and the director has begun. The same can be said of the set designer, who, through the design, may reveal much about the world of the characters and about particular characters. For example, what does a room tell us about its owner? If the director is working with designers, character choices begin to be defined before casting, when the design begins to take shape. If not, the rehearsal process may allow for greater interpretative latitude about each character, for if the costume has not yet been designed or chosen, the actors' choices may inform the costume, instead of the reverse, which is usually the case in the professional theater.

Let's start with a bit of a character warm-up, based on the work of Keith Johnstone in his book *Impro*. This is a simple exercise that can be used in class or rehearsal to get directors and actors to think about how character choices relate to one another and to the other elements of production.

EXERCISE

Perform this improvisation in a circle. Circles tend to have a different energy and power dynamics than other formations. The circle is communal; it encourages equal participation; and it promotes a flow of energy around the circle that is extremely useful in the appropriate situation.

The lead person in this exercise starts by thinking up the name of a character. It may be a silly name (such as a cartoon character might have), like Harry Huckleberry, or a more realistic name, like Janet Fiorelli. Once the name has been chosen, the next person in the circle adds a quality to the name: virtually any distinguishing personal characteristic (physical, psychological, economic, occupational, and so on). Each person in the circle adds another quality until the group agrees that the character has been fully described.

Discussion

1. What characteristics gave the strongest sense of character?

2. What types or categories of characteristics did your group explore? What was neglected?

3. Which characteristics went well together, and which ones seemed to go against the overall flow of the characterization? Did any of the choices seems unusual, but still work?

4. Is there a relationship between characters' names and their characteristics?

This first exercise should help to loosen everyone up and get you all thinking about what characteristics help define a character and how various characteristics may blend together or seem in opposition. I frequently find that characteristics that seem to be in opposition make for more complex, deeper characters. You may find that when the class creates a truly uniform character, the characterization borders on stereotype, whereas a character that embodies apparent inconsistencies, contradictions, or paradoxes seems more real. Different types of plays, depending upon the playwright, the style of the piece, and the period of their writing, use different kinds of characterization, along a continuum from stereotypical to complex to tantalizingly ambiguous. Character analysis helps the director not only understand the characters, but also come to grips with the world of the play and the style of the playwright.

When analyzing character, look for the characteristics the playwright does not provide as well. For example, ancient Greek tragedies rarely contain a great deal of detail about the physical characteristics of the characters. Scholars have suggested some reasons for this. The use of large masks in the ancient Greek theater made the physical qualities of the actors less important than they are now, and placed a much greater emphasis on the actors' vocal qualities and their ability to project. The absence of certain characteristics might reveal as much about character as a stage direction with specific character qualities, for it may place more emphasis on psychological than physical characteristics, or suggest that a character's physicality is less important than his or her moral qualities, for example.

In the next exercises, we will look at text first and extract characteristics from what the playwright describes and implies.

EXERCISE

Using *Betrayal* or your lab play, choose a character for the class to examine together, preferably a character with a large role, to give you the most material with which to work. Pick a significant scene to focus on for your character analysis. You may incorporate information from other parts of the play, but focus on gaining as much character information as you can from the limited information in the scene.

1. Read over the scene individually, making notes in the margins about any indication of character qualities. From this list, select the three most important characteristics that help define your interpretation of the character. Write a paragraph in which you list these three characteristics and argue for their importance.

2. Team up with two other students and pass the statements around in a circle. Discuss (or write) the differences among your interpretations, and how and why they might be significant. You do not have to come to a consensus as to what is most important, but if you agree on the importance of certain characteristics, note these.

3. Come together as a class so that each group may present their findings. Note and discuss the contradictions revealed, as well as whether these must be settled one way or another or if the contradictions add complexity and can therefore be explored.

Discussion

Discuss the different types of characteristics that you've discovered. Compare these with the list below, and discuss why you might have focused on certain traits in this scene instead of others.

Summary of Character Traits for Analysis

Physical: age, gender, race, height, weight, hair and eye color, musculature, internal and external rhythms, body type, distinguishing features, injuries, clothing

Emotional: strengths and weaknesses, needs, coping mechanisms

Psychological: types of thinking, personality type, moral code

Intellectual: natural and learned intelligence, educational background

Social: economic class, occupation, nationality

Ethical/religious: ethical and/or religious beliefs and actions

Political: party affiliation, political system

Relationship and Status

Characters do not exist in a vacuum; they define themselves in **relationship** to those around them. Relationships are always changing, not only over the course of time, but from scene to scene (depending upon who is in the scene, where it occurs, and so on) and from moment to moment within a scene (shifting status in relation to the other characters). Each character, in effect, plays roles within their role. For example, in Pinter's *Betrayal*, Jerry can be seen in terms of his occupation: a successful writers' agent. He could be seen in terms of his family life: a married man with two children. Or his character could be defined by his illicit relationship: his affair with Emma, his best friend's wife. These parts of his character isolate different portions of Jerry's identity within the public and private spheres of his world. His relationships help define his character, for we judge characters not only by the company they keep, but also by the way in which they relate to them.

Likewise, within any given relationship, a character does not always behave the same way. At times, Jerry may feel equal, superior, or inferior to Robert or Emma. A character's **status**—a term Keith Johnstone popularized in his book *Impro*—varies depending upon whom they are with and where they are, and it shifts depending the action of the scene. Johnstone notes that in real life, people who know each other well tend to shift status with each other more frequently, perhaps as a sign of their level of comfort with each other, and characters who don't know each other very well tend to hold one level of status more rigidly. He also observes several other general rules about status that are worth noting here:

- A character's status is not always consistent with his or her occupation. For example, a butler may play high status while a master plays low status.
- High-status characters tend to hold their pauses, "ers," and "ums" longer, an indication that they feel in control and are comfortable taking their time. It is as if they expect people to wait for their next word.
- Characters reveal their status through body language, both their own body language and the way in which they interact with others. High-status characters appear to take up more room, as if their personal space is larger than that of low-status characters (see Figure 4.8), who tend to have small personal spaces or "hug the walls," hence the term "wallflower." High-status characters tend to be more comfortable encroaching upon other characters' spaces or touching them. Think of the implied threat (and high-status comfort level) when a mobster flicks lint or straightens the lapels of someone who owes him money.
- Characters often inadvertently lower their status by trying to play higher status. The highest status players tend to be relaxed because they are comfortable with their status.
- The way characters dress indicates a great deal about their self-perception of their status, and how they would like to be perceived in a particular situation. One study observed that when American presidents enjoy high popularity, they tend to wear their neckties loose and low; when their popularity wanes, they are inclined to tighten up their neckties and wear them higher to try to exhibit a more powerful image.
- Whether the character is in a room that he or she owns or works in tells audiences a great deal about the character's status. Status can be revealed by what chair a character chooses to sit in, whether he or she keeps objects (like a desk) between himself or herself and the other characters, and how familiar he or she is with the objects in the room.
- How a character moves within a space reveals his or her comfort level in the space, personal sense of status, and relationship to the owner of the room.

EXERCISES

1. **Relationship exercise.** Work in pairs with someone in the group who is playing the same character as you in *Betrayal* or your lab play. Write down your analysis of the character's relationships to the other characters in the play, and then compare your conclusions with those of your partner.

FIGURE 4.8 *The Birthday Party* **by Harold Pinter.** Purdue University. In this scene, Goldberg exerts relaxed high status by taking up maximum space without trying hard to do so. McCann must come to Goldberg to ask his advice, so that even though McCann is at a higher level, his status is lower in relationship to Goldberg. Goldberg (sitting): Andrew Persinger. McCann (standing): Adam Kovac.

- To whom is your character closest? Describe three significant aspects of this relationship.
- To whom is your character most antagonistic? Describe three significant aspects of this relationship.
- Examine a character who is mentioned in the play but does not appear on stage. Describe three significant aspects of his or her relationship to your character.

2. **Status exercise.** Examine the scene on which you are working with your scene partner. Write down your analysis of the characters' status interactions and then compare your conclusions with those of your partner.
   - What is the starting and ending status of your character in relationship to your partner's character? What causes the shift?
   - At what points in the scene does your character's status shift and why?
   - At what points is your character most and least vulnerable? How much does this have to do with his or her changing relationship with the other character(s)?

3. On your own (perhaps between classes), chart your character's status progression throughout the scene, marking the exact points at which his or her status changes. Write down a reason for each status shift, and give each section of the scene—as divided up by the status shifts rather than as units of action—a relationship description (i.e., father–daughter, lovers' spat, former best friends).

Discussion

1. How subjective to you, as an actor and as a character, are your character's relationships and status? What are the keys that change the relationship or status?

2. List some examples of dialogue that causes status shifts.

3. What types of physical and vocal behavior tend to accompany status shifts?

4. How do relationships and status provide directors and actors with opportunities to shape the action?

Key Terms
A character's **relationship** to others can be described in terms of a general category, such as mother–son, husband–wife, or best friends. This initial level of analysis is generic, however, since relationships within each category vary greatly. Examine the relationships in your play more closely to find the specifics within a category. For instance, is a particular marriage of long standing, or are the husband and wife newlyweds? How well do they get along? What are the issues in the

relationship? Who makes decisions in particular situations? You should also be sensitive to changes in any given relationship, as the characters' interactions, the social context of a particular scene, and the actions of other characters will change each character's **status** within most relationships. Circumstances and actions change characters' status to one another on an ongoing basis. For example, in *Betrayal*, how does the relationship between Jerry and Emma change when they are in public versus private? How does Emma's pregnancy change the relationship? What happens to the relationship between Robert and Jerry when they stop playing squash, or when Robert first finds out about Jerry's affair with Emma?

Language

We've been looking at language throughout this book. Yet language and dialogue offer the director so much in the way of information and raw material that we're going to look at it again, this time for its broader qualities. From the play's language, we can infer much about the characters, relationships, and action/objectives of the play, yet language functions on another level as well: it suggests sounds, tempos, and rhythms. Language is not only a textual element; it is a visceral element as well. On the page, it is text; on the stage it is shared with the audience. How can an ensemble understand and communicate the textual implications of a play's language while exploring the visceral ways in which it can be handled on stage?

First, let's look at language purely as sound. Different plays and playwrights use language in a wide range of ways. Language can be poetic, as in Shakespearean verse, in rhyme, as in many of Moliére's plays, or realistic, as in Arthur Miller's plays. Language helps create the pulse of a production, the percussive beat of the language driving the play and creating its rhythmic foundation. Many of the plays of David Mamet are characterized as being full of expletives, but his use of cursing often has a rhythmic quality that should not be overlooked. Depending upon where a play is set, the language will have the rhythm of the culture, the economic class, the rural or urban setting, and the characters' professions. Alliteration and assonance (the repetition of consonants and vowels, respectively) create sounds that can be shaped in production. The predominance of certain sounds may suggest certain actions, emotions, and moods. The language of a play, as well as the implied or specified pauses, may also suggest tempos that create an overall rhythm for the production moment to moment. The character's words tell you a great deal about who they are, how they relate to others in the scene, and what they want.

EXERCISES

1. Select a scene set in a public space, such as scene one in *Betrayal*. Write down the most frequently used voiced sounds in the scene (the sounds most common within the dialogue). What do these sounds tell you

about the character, economic class, relationship, and actions of the scene? How does the environment support or contrast with the language? Pair up with a partner and come to an agreement as to the most revealing language in the scene.

2. Using the same scene, what language choices reveal the most about the tempo and rhythm of the scene? With your partner, isolate three language choices that appear to suggest the controlling rhythms and tempos of the scene.

3. What does the characters' use of language reveal about their characters and the central conflict of the scene?

4. Compare the language in the scene you have been examining to another scene in which the characters' circumstances differ greatly. For example, you could compare scene one of *Betrayal* (in which Emma and Jerry meet two years after their affair) to scene four (in which Robert is present as well), scene seven (early in the affair), or scene nine (when Jerry makes his interest known to Emma). What does the characters' use of language reveal about their state of mind, their actions and objectives, and the tempo and rhythm of the scenes?

Summary

Language may reveal any of the following characteristics of the play or characters: economic class, rhythm and tempo, the style of the play, the setting of the play, the culture of the world of the play, and the relationships and status of the characters in the scene. As language finds its ultimate expression and interpretation through the actors, who give life to the words and intentions to the action, it serves to bridge the gap between textual and visual directing elements. How the actors give voice to the playwright's words will be a central determinant to the rhythm and tempo of the production as well. For this reason, although we can look at the content of a play's language to reveal its possibilities in production, how the language is handled will shape the action on stage greatly. As you work on the exercises in the next section, "Visceral Elements," seek to integrate the skills you acquire with the textual elements you've been working on. The visceral elements of directing are the physical, visual, and aural means by which you realize your interpretation of the core action of a play.

Visceral Elements

The visceral elements of directing shape the production by giving concrete form to the text. They may appear to be clear physical manifestations of the text, as when a character says and does the same thing, or visceral elements may be in direct conflict with the text, as when a character says one thing and does another. Language serves as an interesting bridge between the text and the staging, since the words a character speaks can be completely opposed to his or her actions, rhythms, and body language. Similarly, the actors' and director's decisions about the intention of a moment in a play may clarify the moment or open it to further ambiguity. For example, in scene three of *Betrayal*, when Jerry says, "I don't think we don't love each other," his double negative creates ambiguity. Does he mean to say "I love you," or has he been reduced to merely refuting Emma's charges? This could be a confused statement of love, delivered with open arms and warm vocal tones. Or Jerry could be in fighting mode: arms crossed, maximum distance from Emma, and speaking in a harsh voice. Thus, textual elements are never is concrete as they appear, and visceral elements are the major way in which a director realizes his or her interpretation of the text.

Tempo and Rhythm

Tempo is the speed of the overall production or any part of it. You can describe this in any number of ways. Some directors use the musical terms (most of which originate from Italian) for tempo, such *largo* (slowly), *andante* (moderate), *allegro* (lively), *agitato* (agitated), and *presto* (very quickly). Others prefer to describe tempo in everyday language, as simply fast, medium, slow, or somewhere in between. Some directors even mark the tempo with a metronome: 100 beats per minute, for example. Occasionally, directors beat out the tempo with a pencil on their rehearsal table, as a way of setting the pace of a scene or encouraging the actors to speed up or slow down. Tempo can reflect a sense of real time, or by slowing or speeding up the tempo, the ensemble can create a sense of stylized reality (see Figure 4.9).

You should also be aware of the term **pace** or **pacing**, which is often used interchangeably with tempo, but actually has a slightly different meaning. Tempo refers to speed; pace or pacing implies a sense of thrust or impulse in a scene. A scene may have three tempos in it—a slow first unit, a quick second unit, and a moderate third unit, for example—but the overall pacing of the scene must connect these three distinct tempos. Tempo dictates a single speed, whereas pace includes several speeds within the entire unit, scene, or act. A production with good pacing will appear to be seamless, as the pacing will bridge the transitions between different tempos. Pacing is subjective; it may differ from place to place and production to production, depending upon the audience and the director's individual taste.

Rhythm is a bit more complex than tempo, and a bit more specific and easier to describe than pacing. It is the *pattern* of the beat of a scene or the overall production. You can think of rhythm, particularly on the larger level of the production, as being made up of a series of tempos that create a pattern. For example, if we were examining the rhythm of a five-scene play, we might find that the first four scenes are progressively faster, followed by a slow fifth scene. We might

FIGURE 4.9 *Body Beautiful* **by Naomi Iizuka.** Theater North Collaborative, NYC. Completely symmetrical, identical images often lend a stylized sense of altered reality to a moment. In this play, two women obsessed with losing weight chose to have multiple elective surgeries. The stylized moment in this scene was further accentuated by extending time. Underscored by abstract, spacey music, the two women took one full minute to each bring a single M&M to her mouth. Ariance Brandt (left) and Calista Flockhart (right).

find that the scenes alternate between faster and slower ones, with an overall build. Using only words at this point, we could describe the rhythm these two interpretations of the five scenes as:

> Interpretation #1: Slow—medium—moderately fast—rapid—very slow
> Interpretation #2: Slow—moderately fast—medium—rapid—very slow

You can see just from this simple example how different choices of tempo for each scene produce a different overall rhythm for the production.

On a smaller level, rhythm may be described in slightly different ways. Some directors talk about the beat. For example, "This scene has a driving beat," or "The rhythm of this scene is slow and sedate, until the entrance of the third character, who disrupts the peacefulness of the rhythm with his violent energy."

It's also possible to drum out the rhythm with a pencil in the same way you would a tempo, simply adding a pattern: two slow taps, followed by three fast ones, and so on. We're going to look at some sample scenes and try to explore their possible tempos and rhythms.

EXERCISES

1. Explore the range of possible tempos of scene four in Betrayal or a scene in your lab play. Scene four has several entrances and exits from offstage, which tend to mark distinct tempo changes. Working with teams of two or three, quickly break the scene down into four to six playable units. On your own, assign each unit a tempo. Compare your tempos to those of your partners, agree on the terminology you will use to describe tempo, and then attempt to come to a consensus about the tempo of each unit. How does tempo relate to the action of the scene? Do your tempo choices reflect differing opinions about the action and characters, or do you simply hear the dialogue in your head in different ways? If the latter, does your ear for the scene, upon further consideration, reflect your attitude toward the characters or action?

2. There are other ways to capture or describe the tempo/rhythm of a scene. Work on your directing scene at home, without discussing it with your scene partner, and find a piece of music that captures your sense of the tempo and rhythm of each unit. Play the music for your class, explaining its connection to each unit. How do your choices compare with those of your partner? This exercise has a practical application as well. You might use the music to underscore the scene in production, or use it as underscoring in rehearsal to help establish the tempos and rhythms.

Key Terms

- **Tempo** is the speed of a scene or unit. It may be described in any language that captures the sense of the speed, including music terminology, beats per minute, or by playing music.
- **Rhythm** is the pattern of a unit, scene, or play. It can be used to describe the pulse of a unit or the overall pattern created from scene to scene throughout a play. Rhythm therefore can be described on many levels: from the smallest (the rhythm of a page or less of dialogue) to the largest (the overall rhythm of the play).

Sound and Mood

Sound and mood go hand in hand, because sound is an important element in creating mood and is also a consequence of mood. Imagine, if you will, a peaceful early morning by the ocean. What are the sounds you might hear? How much do these sounds contribute to the mood of the scene? Although it is true that you can also attribute the sounds to the environment, there are a great many possible sounds in the environment that could change the mood. For example, is the ocean peaceful or stormy? Are the seagulls relatively quiet or squawking for food? Are there other sounds in the environment that might shift the mood, such as passing cars or a speedboat?

In addition to selecting sounds from the given environment, the director can also add background sounds or music. Sound that plays within a scene may be motivated by the environment itself—music such as a jukebox playing in a diner or sounds such as crickets, birds, traffic—in which case the sound would be essentially realistic. This is called **environmental sound**. Or the sound or music may be added by the director purely as an element of the style of the production, in which case we refer to it as **underscoring**. Sound can be recorded and played on the theater's sound system (or on a portable CD player, if the production is played in a found space) or may be made by some or all members of the ensemble during the performance, such as when actors sing a song, chant, or create other sounds. Again, these sounds can be realistic or stylized, depending upon the vision of the director.

For a developing director, sound is perhaps the least expensive design element to complement the production and help shape the action, as well as the easiest to control. With CD burners standard on most computers and simple sound design software pre-installed as well, almost anyone can burn a CD with a set of sound cues for a production at almost no cost. As you develop as a director, you may have the opportunity to work with sound engineers, who will produce sounds for your production, or sound designers, who will collaborate on the sound for a production with you. But until you have the luxury of a sound designer, it will be up to you to provide sound for your productions, and there is little reason not to avail yourself of this powerful design element.

Sound can also be a powerful element in making transitions between scenes. Rather than allow the transition time to be filled by the sounds of actors entering and exiting or stagehands moving furniture, transitions provide you with an opportunity to bridge the gap between the scenes. You may decide to use this opportunity to punctuate the end of the previous scene or to set up the mood for the scene to follow. Silence is still an option, but this is a choice that you make, and one that will be most powerful if it is chosen for a reason, either in contrast to the sound between other scenes or as an overall motif tied to your vision of the production.

EXERCISES

1. Look over scene nine from Betrayal for possible sound cues, or examine a scene from another play that has offstage sounds invading the stage space with each entrance or exit. What does the script imply about the use of sound in production? Pick two moments in the scene that could

be augmented with sound: one with environmentally motivated music, and one with environmentally motivated sound. Explain in writing how these cues contribute to the mood and shape of the scene. Exchange your explanation with another director in the class, and respond back and forth to each other's ideas until you reach agreement or impasse. Where would you choose to locate the source of the sound for maximum effectiveness?

2. Select any two sequential scenes in your lab play and experiment with music or sound that could be used to help make the transition between scenes. Bring into class a recording of the sound you find most effective for making the transition, and discuss your reasons for choosing it.

Key Terms

- **Environmental sound** is any sound that can be justified by the environment that the playwright specifies or the production chooses as a setting. For example, for a restaurant setting environmental sound might include background conversations, music, the opening and closing of doors, and kitchen sounds. For a beach scene, environmental sounds might include the ocean, other weather-related sounds such as a storm or wind, and adults, children, or animals playing on the beach or in the water. Even if environmental sound is specified in the script, the director can control the type of sound used, its volume, and when it occurs within the scene.
- **Stylized sound** occurs when the script calls for it or the director adds sound that does not occur naturally in the setting. This may be **underscoring** (see below) for mood or may involve more aggressive uses of sound. As with any design element, the director should seek to use stylized sound in a way that helps shape the action and is consistent with the overall interpretation of the play.
- **Underscoring** is the use of music underneath the spoken dialogue; in other words, music that can be heard without obscuring the actors' dialogue. The level of the sound is an important choice for the director when using underscoring, as it can help bring the actors down to a whisper or raise their voices to a scream. Underscoring can also be a useful rehearsal technique; by playing music in rehearsal, the director can establish a mood, tempo, and rhythm for the action and influence the actors indirectly, but powerfully.
- **Ensemble-created sound** refers to those that the actors or crew make themselves, through the use of their voices, bodies, instruments, or percussion.
- **Transitions** between scenes provide the director with opportunities to bridge the gap from one moment to another.
- The **sound plot** is a written set of sound cues for a production, with specific notations as to when each sound cue will be called during each scene.

Visual Composition

We will refer to the placement of actors on the stage in relationship to one another, the set, and the audience as **visual composition**. Just as created and recorded sounds give shape to the listening experience of a theater production— an aural composition, akin to the rhythms of a radio drama—the placement of the actors from moment to moment creates a series of visual pictures that help establish the rhythm or shape of the production. In their book *Fundamentals of Play Directing*, Alexander Dean and Lawrence Carra describe visual composition in terms of **composition** (the placement of the actors) and **picturization** (the story that the composition suggests). This division, however, suggests that composition is a technical matter that involves placing actors in certain preferred positions, and its primary aim is storytelling, which it achieves through the pictures the director creates. Although these concepts are valid and useful to understand, we might also look at composition as part of the overall fabric of the production, one that is created collaboratively with the entire ensemble. Whereas it will be useful to understand how composition helps tell stories and make balanced stage pictures, we're going to focus on how to create compositions that will help shape the production collaboratively.

First, recognize that the groundplan suggests certain compositions, so in effect the groundplan that you develop on your own or with a designer will open up certain types of compositions and curtail others. For example, the placement of the chairs will suggest certain seating arrangements; doorways will set the angle of entries and exits; all properties on stage will require actors to move around them in certain patterns. The possible range of compositions will offer you opportunities to color the narrative in certain ways.

Every day, the groundplans within our environment affect our compositions and patterns of movement (we'll look at this in the next section, "Movement"). For example, when someone gets into an elevator, he or she tends to face the door; when a second person enters the elevator, the first person adjusts position. The technical term for this movement in theater is "to counter." Thus, a director might say, "When the second actor comes in to this scene, I want the first actor to **counter** to the left." In life, then, our environment suggests compositions. Picturization works in the opposite direction: The composition suggests a story or situation. For example, we might assume that two people sitting side by side on a park bench are lovers or old friends, depending upon their specific body positions. In this way, groundplan affects composition, composition helps interpret narrative, and narrative is shaped by composition and put into motion through movement.

Audiences view compositions within a literal or implied **frame**. Frames very greatly in size and shape, and stage configurations alter an audience's sensitivity to the frame. Proscenium staging, in which the audience is on one side and the performers on the opposite side of the entire theater space, draws its name from the proscenium arch, which, in its most ornate forms, consists of a visible and frequently elaborate frame around the action, similar to a frame for a painting. The proscenium frame tends to be the most visible and noticeable to the audience. Thrust staging, in which the audience is on three sides of the action, whether fully or partially surrounding the action on three sides, can utilize a visible frame (from which the action may extend into the audience by using an apron: an extension of the stage that pushes past the boundaries of the frame), or it can use a less visible frame or none at all. Arena staging, in which the audience is on all four sides of the action, implicitly uses its audience to frame the action, as they contain the performing space on all sides. Environmental staging, in which actors and audience co-mingle, frequently plays with the boundaries of the frame, allowing actors to cross these borders between actor and audience and therefore violate or alter the frame during the course of the production.

Within any frame, compositions may be symmetrical or asymmetrical; both have their place in effective stage compositions. **Symmetrical compositions**, in which the characters are perfectly balanced and the overall composition forms a visible and regular pattern, tend to imply a sense of order or formality (see Figure 4.10), frequently implying a social order or hierarchy. **Asymmetrical compositions**, in which the characters' positions do not form a symmetrical pattern but may still find balance through angles, variety, and relative weight, tend to be more dynamic and less formal (see Figure 4.11). If unbalanced, an asymmetrical composition may suggest disorder or chaos. The two can be used exclusively, but more frequently are used in contrast to one another. Sometimes such contrasts are implied in the script, as in *King Lear*, when the formal, symmetrical division of the kingdom by Lear in Act I, scene 2, could be proceeded by an asymmetrical composition for the scene in which Gloucester introduces his bastard son Edmund to Kent, a contrast that Gloucester's bawdy language only reinforces.

EXERCISES

1. **Framing and filling**. Collaborating in groups of three or four, select a found environment and, by process of discussion and consensus, choose the most powerful frame and angle on the space. Examine these spaces as a class and discuss them. What makes the visual dynamics of each space particularly powerful at that angle? Working as individuals, imagine filling the frame with two or three bodies. Compare everyone's compositions within each space and frame, using volunteers from your class as the "characters" within the space. What do you notice about the different compositions? What opportunities do the space and angle provide for alternatives? Is this a space that encourages the director to compose in a wide variety of ways?

2. **Composing in found environments.** Go to a building nearby that has a wide variety of spaces, both inside and out, within which a director could create a visual composition. Each director should explore the building and find a space within it that could contain a visual composition made up of two or three bodies placed within the space. If need be, you can experiment with compositions with more than three bodies, although

FIGURE 4.10 *Hedda Gabler* **by Henrik Ibsen.** This composition effectively uses a symmetrical composition and a frame in the background (a literal picture frame that serves as the wall between Hedda's drawing room and the rest of the downstairs). The picturization of this composition helps tell the story: In the foreground, Thea implores Eilert not to drink again, while Hedda stands between them, in the background, jealously glaring her disapproval. Scene design: Tim Golebiewski. Thea: Ashleigh Catsos. Hedda: Kristin Knapp. Eilert: Daniel Leary.

FIGURE 4.11 *Twelfth Night* **by William Shakespeare.** Slightly asymmetrical, balanced composition, as Cesario/Viola (Athena Fitzpatrick) tries to figure out which woman is Olivia. Scene Design: Takeshi Kata. Lighting Design: Matt Richards.

you might find it more productive to start with smaller groups of two or three and then repeat the exercise with larger groups to build on the skills you acquire. Imagine the composition in detail, thinking not only about where you would place each body, but also about their bodily positions and their relationships to one another. Allow the space to suggest possibilities, rather than looking for a space in which to stage a preconceived idea. Reassemble as a class and move from space to space in the building, with each director creating their composition using their colleagues' bodies. What creates a strong visual composition? How important is the weight of bodies in different parts of the composition? How would you frame the composition for maximum effect? Does the composition tell a story? How would a change in the composition alter the story or create a more dynamic image? Discuss what you learned from the exercise and isolate basic concepts of visual composition that seem to affect the director's visual work consistently.

Key Terms

- **Visual composition** is the art and craft of placing bodies within the confines of a theatrical space. If the director has a full team of designers working on a production, visual composition involves the director collaborating with the designers to create spaces, silhouettes, and lighting looks that unite to form a complete picture, within which the director collaborates with actors in creating the compositions.

- **Countering** refers to the convention of actors balancing their stage positions in reaction to the entrance or movement of another actor or group of actors on stage. It contributes greatly to the ability to move from composition to composition smoothly.

- **Picturization** occurs when the visual composition of a scene conveys a situation, relationship, or story by virtue of its composition. Picturization can convey story and relationship, whether the director preplans the composition or discovers with the ensemble in rehearsal.

- The **frame** of any composition is created by any device that delineates a portion of the stage area as the playing space. The most apparent frame is a proscenium arch, which serves as a literal picture frame around the action. The frame of a composition is always a factor, whether observed formally, broken purposefully, or alternated for effect.

- **Balanced compositions** find equilibrium through the placement of the relative weights of different objects and people on stage. Not every composition needs to be balanced, but directors should always be aware of the effect of the balance or imbalance of a composition on the shape of the action. Asymetrical compositions can still find balance through a combination of the weight and number of forms on stage. For example, a single large form upstage left might be balanced by several small forms downstage right—asymmetrical, but balanced.

- **Symmetrical compositions** exhibit a visual pattern and tend to imply formality, as in a courtroom or a military formation.

- **Asymmetrical composition** can be balanced or skewed, depending upon whether the weight of different sections of the stage has a sense of equilibrium. Directors use asymmetrical compositions for variety; unbalanced asymmetry tends to imply disorder or chaos, as when an unruly gang storms a place or attacks an individual.

- **Dynamic composition** refers to the interest created by the use of angles, levels, and positional tension in your composition. Flat compositions—in which several actors stand in a horizontal line, for example, tend not to be dynamic, though such compositions may be appropriate for particular scenes. Dynamic compositions tend to make greater use of angles, or irregular triangles created by several characters or groups, and of actors standing on different levels or creating levels by virtue of some characters sitting and others standing.

- **Found space** refers to the use of an existing environment for a play or scene. Many significant experimental theater productions have been performed in found spaces (see Figure 4.12), which add an element of reality that can support or contrast the play's action.

Movement

I have chosen to use the word "movement" for this section over the long-standing term "blocking." Historically, the first directors used "blocking" to communicate how their actors should move among the different "blocks" of a stage, having traditionally divided up the stage into nine to fifteen areas. Each block had a name based upon combinations of the fundamental stage notation of stage left and right, downstage, center stage, and upstage. The terminology usually refers to a proscenium stage; for there to be a stage right, the stage has to have a reference point (the audience). Thus, stage right is the right hand side of the stage

FIGURE 4.12 *The Old Woman Broods* by **Tadeusz Rózewicz.** Directed and space design by Kazimierz Braun. The Osterwa Theater, Lublin, Poland. A scene played in a found space in a courtyard near the theater building. Zbigniew Górski as the Poet, with spectators below. Photo courtesy of Kazimierz Braun.

from the actors' point of view as they face the audience. This notation also works fairly well with a thrust configuration, but it does not work in arena staging (with the audience on all four sides) or environmental staging (where the audience is not in one distinct area), although any stage area could be divided up into blocks or areas for the sake of writing down the movement. The notebooks Stanislavski prepared prior to rehearsing his early productions of Anton Chekhov's plays graphically reveal the extent to which he preblocked his actor's movements and even minute gestures prior to the first rehearsal.

Because the history of the term is tied to the tradition of the director pre-blocking the actors' movements—in other words, blocking refers to *planned* stage movement—I prefer to use the more straightforward word "movement," which to me sheds the implication that the director makes all decisions about the actors' movements. Some directors still preblock the entire production, others work off movement the actors develop in rehearsal, and many directors combine these approaches. Regardless of how movement is developed in rehearsal, the director is ultimately responsible for selecting, suggesting, and altering the actors' movements to maximize their effectiveness in production on a particular stage and set. The actors' movements need not be preplanned, but they must be effective at communicating the essence of the scene in a particular setting and production.

We will be working on two sets of movement skills for the director: the development of your perception of effective movement on stage and the ability to collaborate on movement with your ensemble. Movement serves many purposes in a production. Good movement allows the actors to make smooth transitions between major compositional moments. If you and your ensemble find that one key moment of a play finds its ultimate expression in a particular composition, movement should carry you to the composition of the next key moment with seemingly little effort. Movement can help interpret the action of the play. For example, what do we perceive differently about the interaction between two characters when one walks away from the other? What if they both walk toward each other? How might the pace of their movements change our perception?

Movement also contributes to the shape and rhythm of a production. You and the ensemble create patterns of bodies on stage through choices of movement, and the pace of the movements contributes to the rhythm and tempo of the scene and the overall play. Movement can reveal a great deal about the environment and the characters' respective places in it. The types of movement that occur within an environment tell you a great deal about this world; the characters' relationships to one another may also be revealed through movement. Movement defines territories, revealing to whom the space belongs and the status of visitors. It can also help to define the space as public or private.

In a scene with minimal movement, the smallest movements take on great significance. Directors refer to these small movements as **business**, particularly when the movements involve an object, as when lighting a cigarette or arranging flowers. This kind of detail can add detail and character to a scene, so long as it isn't overdone (see Figure 4.13). When a scene occurs at a table, for example, the

script may indicate that the characters do not leave the table for an extended period of time. This does not mean that the director is freed from collaborating
with the actors on movement, but rather that the smallest movements take on
greater significance. When a scene is played in a small area, as when two or more
characters engage in extended dialogue at a table, it is the theatrical equivalent to
a medium or close-up shot in film. The "frame" for the physical action has become smaller, and therefore what may seem to be an insignificant movement in
a larger frame will have enormous impact, as when a character in a table scene
leans forward or back, crosses his or her legs and turns to the side, or looks away.
When you block intimate spatial scenes, think cinematically, and therefore work
within a much smaller compositional frame.

Adding "business" to a scene, as in scene seven of *Betrayal* when Robert repeatedly pours himself more wine, can help reveal his tension and his inner feelings, and contribute to the pacing of the scene. In this way, in a theatrical
"close-up" scene, business is the equivalent to larger movements in a scene that

FIGURE 4.13 *Waco Woman* **by Linda McDonald.** Circle Rep Lab, NYC. In this
play about a female impersonator, the most important props and stage business
revolved around the lead's wigs, a vital part of the character's act and identity. Josh
Pais and Camryn Manheim.

use more of the stage, just as small body position shifts are the same as changes in the visual composition of a larger scene. Focus on the size of the frame within which the scene's actions occur as if a camera, or perhaps indeed the lighting, has isolated the playing area. Movements and compositions will have power depending upon their relative size within the frame.

EXERCISES

1. **Territory exercise**. Pick a scene from *Betrayal* that is set in either Robert and Emma's house, Jerry and Emma's flat, or Jerry's study. Working in a large group or a smaller set of groups, draw a groundplan for the space. What spatial elements or set pieces indicate to whom the territory belongs? Do particular areas of the territory more strongly belong to a particular character? Set up the space and have two or three characters move around in it. What movements support or undercut the owner's claim to the space?

2. **Public space exercise (large frame)**. Examine scene one or five in *Betrayal* or a scene from another play with a public setting. In small or large groups, set up a groundplan for the space. Focus on the entire stage space. How does a public environment affect movement? What factors in the script or in your interpretation of the characters might indicate that the space belongs to one character more than another? How does the presence of other people in the space, whether actual or implied, affect the characters' movement or behavior?

3. **Table scene exercise (small frame)**. Reexamine scenes one and five, paying particular attention to small movements clearly at the table. In a "table scene," in which two or more characters sit at a table and talk, what elements of movement contribute to the scene? Set up one of these scenes around a table, and experiment with as many ways as you can imagine for using movement to help shape the scene and clarify your intention for it.

Summary

- *Private space* usually belongs to one character or is a battleground for characters. How you define a private space communicates on a subconscious level to both the actors and the audience, telling them whose territory it is, as well as how they feel about the space.
- *Public space* operates according to the rules of the society in which it exists, as well as the rules of the function for which it has been designed. Characters may follow or break these rules, purposefully or by accident, and their behavior reveals a lot about the character's position in that world at that given moment.

■ *Entrances and exits* provide the playwright with opportunities to interrupt the flow of a scene and alter the patterns of movement. They provide the director and actors with moments to interpret and shape the action.

Gesture

Each character's gestures function on a number of levels in any given play. On the largest level, gestures reveal a great deal of information about the world of the play and its period setting. For example, how do characters hold themselves, how do they use their hands, and what gestures are accepted in this world? On the level of the individual character, do their gestures fit within this world or do they stand out? Do they follow the rules of this society? If they reject the rules, do they do so purposefully or from a lack of knowledge of society's customs? How do their gestures position them in society: as an outsider, an insider, or a rebel or clown?

When the late President Nixon was vice president to President Eisenhower in the 1950s, he traveled the world on diplomatic assignments. During a visit to a Latin American country, Nixon held both arms above his head with his middle and pointer fingers raised in a "V" upon emerging from his airplane. Although this would later become Nixon's trademark gesture for victory during his 1968 presidential campaign, in this particular country, the awaiting dignitaries and citizens reacted with shock and revulsion. Little did Nixon know that this sign had the same meaning as if he had raised his middle finger to a crowd of Americans. Needless to say, his gesture marked an inauspicious beginning to his visit. What gestures have specific meanings in your city, school, or circle of friends? In the world of any given play, what does a gesture signify?

On the level of the individual, gestures become personal: a sign of the character's identity and self-concept. Comic impressionists understand that a single gesture can evoke a person and reflect the dominance of a particular aspect of someone's character. In addition to copying a person's voice, most comic impressionists repeatedly use a trademark gesture for each person they imitate. President Clinton was known for gesturing with his right thumb extending from a clenched fist; President Reagan was most famous for tilting his head to the side for a moment, usually accompanied by one of his most famous lines, "There you go again." And comedian Rich Little made President's Nixon's jowls a prominent part of his impression, by shaking his cheeks as he said, "I am not a crook."

EXERCISES

1 **Impressions.** Watch a television show or the news and try to isolate one well-known person's most prevalent or revealing gesture. What does the gesture say about the character and his or her place in their world? Is it a personal, societal, or psychological gesture? Is the character or person aware of the gesture, or does it come out unconsciously? Perform

the gesture silently for the class, and see if they can guess who you are imitating and interpret the meaning of the gesture.

2. **Social circles.** Observe a group of people on campus or in your town or city to isolate a single gesture that several people use. What is the purpose of this gesture: group identification, humor, or some other form of communication? Discuss the meaning of these gestures with your class.

3. **Approval, rejection, and indifference.** Think about your character in the scene you are working on. What unique gestures might he or she use to indicate approval, rejection, and indifference? Compare your gestures to your partner's. What does the contrast or similarity tell you about the characters? What would be the effect of your character copying or sharing a gesture with the other character?

Key Terms

- **Personal gestures** are unique to the individual. They may be accepted within the world of a play as a distinguishing characteristic or as a sign of the character's outsider status.
- Michael Chekhov, a disciple of Konstantin Stanislavski, focused a great deal of his acting work and teaching on what he referred to as the **psychological gesture**. Such a gesture captures something essential about the character and can be used to unlock a deeper understanding of the character or stronger emotions.
- Bertolt Brecht coined the term *gestus* to indicate gestures that revealed the significance of a scene or a particular action. In Brechtian acting, the gestus is bold and obvious—an acting choice that brings attention to itself.
- If a group shares a common gesture among its members, it may carry a greater meaning as a **societal gesture**. When the Duke University basketball players all slap the floor as they go back on defense during a game, they signal each other that it's time to play tight defense. Such a gesture helps solidify the group, while at the same time serving to intimidate their opponents.

Environment

There are many ways to think about the *environment* or world of a play. The text itself may describe physical, social, political, or psychological elements of the setting in great detail, depending upon the playwright's preferences and the norms of the time and place in which it was written. Environmental elements may be specified in the stage directions or implied in the dialogue. Shakespeare wrote almost no stage directions, but his characters refer to their environments throughout the dialogue. Some of the most prominent American playwrights of the twentieth century, such as Arthur Miller, Eugene O'Neill, and Tennessee

Williams, wrote voluminous notes on all aspects of the environment surrounding the action. This trend began in the late-nineteenth century, influenced by the psychological theories of Sigmund Freud and the behavioral theories of Darwin, who each contributed to the Western view that environment creates behavior and influences character. Early realistic and naturalistic plays attempted to demonstrate the relationship between environment and character. Emile Zola's theories of naturalism encouraged playwrights to capture a "slice of life" on stage that would display the multiplicity of environmental factors contributing to the development of a character or group. Realistic playwrights tended to reduce these factors to their essentials, so that a few major environmental factors appear in strong relief. The major European playwrights of the late nineteenth century, such as Henrik Ibsen (*A Doll House, Hedda Gabler*), August Strindberg (*Miss Julie*), and Anton Chekhov (*The Three Sisters, Uncle Vanya, The Cherry Orchard*) all experimented with the power of environmental factors in many of their most acclaimed plays.

At the same time, beginning with the work of the duke of Saxe-Meiningen, directors started to employ design elements, with the help of their designers, to create stage environments that reflected or reinforced the playwrights' concerns. Saxe-Meiningen placed real trees on stage for one production; at the Théâtre Libré, André Antoine used real carcasses of beef for a production of *The Butcher*; and for the early productions of Chekhov's plays at the Moscow Art Theater, Konstantin Stanislavski developed extensive notes on environmental sound before starting rehearsals.

In the latter half of the twentieth century, many more aggressive directors altered the environments of plays to support their own concepts of plays, their actions, and their characters' motivations. This type of approach, still in use and most prevalent in contemporary productions of Shakespeare, may alter a play in ways that the playwright may not have intended or the text may not support. Among the directors best known for this approach are Peter Sellars, whose opera productions include *Don Giovanni* set in Spanish Harlem and *Cosi Fan Tutti* set in a diner; the environmental productions of the Wooster Group, whose own plays sometimes included large excerpts from other plays; and Joanne Akalaitis, who set Samuel Beckett's *Endgame* in an abandoned New York subway, a production that triggered a lawsuit by Beckett to close the production.

Contemporary directors find themselves confronted by a large range of choices for environment, since the director is no longer confined by the specifics of the text—at least not after the first professional production. More aggressive directors see the play's setting and environment as an artistic choice, whereas more conservative directors may believe fervently that productions should follow the playwright's intentions as literally as possible. Developing directors should be aware that environment is an artistic choice, so long as it serves the interpretation of the particular production. As a contemporary director, you have some fundamental responsibilities: to understand the playwright's given environment before changing it and to collaborate with any living playwright with whom you work. Yet you have unprecedented freedom, since the only checks on your artistic choices are your collaborators, the producer or theater, the critics, the audience, and your own artistic style and taste.

EXERCISES

1. Examine a scene from *Betrayal* or your lab play, and write down as many environmental factors specified or implied in the text as you can find. On the basis of this information, try to capture the most significant aspects of the environment in three to five sentences. Working with a partner, exchange your conclusions, trading written comments until you arrive at a mutually acceptable set of statements about the environment or can specify the essential differences in your points of view.

2. Select a setting for the play different from what the playwright indicates. Make two columns: one for the original setting and one for your new setting. Under each heading, list the different aspects of the environment that would be required to create that world consistently. Discuss some of these new settings and environments as a class. Is consistency necessary for every play or production? What is the relationship between the environmental facts that the playwright provides and the interpretation that the director employs? Are environmental elements always seen on stage?

Summary

- *Environment* is the world of the production, both seen and unseen. It informs the actions of the characters as well as the audience's view of them. It may be specifically identified in the stage directions, implied in the text, or created by the director and the ensemble.
- The *physical environment* consists of everything that is seen on stage, including personal effects, sounds, structures: anything that involves the five senses.
- The *social environment* is generally not visible, reflected instead by the social norms of the world. It has a major effect upon the characters' behaviors, their opinions about one another, and the audience's views about them.
- The *political environment* is often, but not always, a major factor in the overall world of the play. The director might need to do dramaturgical research into the setting of the play to fully comprehend the politics of the world, particularly if the time period or place is foreign to him or her. Armed with this information, the director must judge how great a part the political environment plays in the characters' beliefs and actions.

Style

Perhaps the most allusive element of shape is style. **Style** encompasses all that brings the world of the play together: the words, the manners, the environment, gestures, movement, sounds, relationships, and even the overall rhythm. As the director builds the values of a production, a style may emerge or these choices may be made to contribute to the style. Much of this depends upon your working method, your collaborators, and the text. When we speak of style of as element of shape, it is not the style in which you direct—how you work, for instance—that we are talking about. Style is essentially the sum of all of the elements of shape that you've acquired some knowledge of through your work thus far.

One way to think of style is by genre. We tend to think of different genres of theater, television, and film as conjuring up a certain style. For example, "soap opera" may imply a style that is preoccupied with the external show of emotion. "Farce" may suggest physicality, a quickening pace, and a sense that the stakes, though high, are ultimately without consequence. All of us make certain assumptions about different genres. What is most important, though, is not how we define a particular genre, but how one assumption about it leads to others. Style works in the same way: One decision triggers another.

EXERCISES

1. **Genre improvisation.** This exercise can be done as a large group or in smaller groups of three to five. On a small slip of paper, write down the name of a genre, such as soap opera, farce, or kabuki. Using a scene from your lab play, pick a slip of paper and act out the scene in that style. Those watching the exercise can write down or note the various elements of that style or genre that emerge from the exercise. This exercise is a staple of improvisation troupes. Once the players have grasped the essential elements of most genres, any scene can be improvised in any style, usually to great laughter. This exercise can be used to get actors to abandon assumptions about material (such as "Shakespeare is high literature" or "Chekhov is depressing") or to see what a completely different take on a text helps the actors discover.

2. Examine another scene from your lab play for elements that suggest an overall style of production that you might like to explore. List three to five essential decisions that you would have to make as a director to achieve the style. Discuss these decisions as a class. How many of them remain consistent from style to style? What is central to the play, and what is essential to the style? Can a stylistic choice undercut fundamental aspects of the text?

Summary
Style is the sum of all elements of production, which gives any production an overall look, feeling, and sensibility. When discovering the style of a production, the director can learn a lot from the text, the playwright's use of language, and the original setting of the play, even if the director eventually decides to alter some of these aspects in the final production.

Integrating Directing Elements

Now that you've experimented with a variety of directing elements, both textual and visceral, and acquired a number of ways of interpreting these elements in rehearsal and production, let's examine one unit from the play we began to analyze in Chapter 2, *The New Rules*. Here is a sample script analysis for the unit, followed by a brief outline that a director might follow in analyzing the entire play and researching the dramaturgical background necessary to fully understand the play.

Sample Unit Score from *The New Rules*

(Analysis appears in italics; text in roman type)

#1 has been away while changes were made to his world. He's relaxed, tanned, calm, and refreshed from vacation.

#2 has been on edge and alone for several weeks, perhaps months. He's anxious, frightened of the slightest sound, and near his breaking point.

Relationship*: #1 and #2 are strangers who share the same occupation: human test subjects. Up until recently, they have taken the routine of their jobs for granted.*

Status: *#1 feels superior because he's been on vacation. #2 feels superior because he knows what's changed since #1 left, although his status has been lowered by his accumulated anxiety. Thus, the scene is a status battle: #1's blissful ignorance at the start shattered by the truth of #2's sense of his imminent demise.*

Unit 2: "It's the new rules."

Actions/objectives:
#1 wants to question #2 for reassurance
#2 wants to torture #1 so he'll share his anxiety.

Subunit A
Rhythm: *#1 easygoing and smooth; #2 jabbing, sharp*
Tempo: *starts off medium-slow*

> **#1:** You so sure? How come? What's new?
>
>   (S) *new info → #2 **shocks** #1*
>
> **#2:** Nothing's happened for months.
>
> **#1:** What do you mean?

#2:   It's the new rules.

            After beat, **tempo** *speeds up* $\left(S\right)$ *Realization →* **#1 begs** *#2*

#1:   (Beat.) What do you mean? There's no longer—

#2:   Any specific time that—

#1:   You know something's going to happen?

                      Tempo *settles down again*

#2:   Right.

Subunit B: "Every Tuesday at two . . ."
Rhythm: *dovetailing, completing each other's thoughts*
Tempo: *accelerates to rapid-fire*

              $\left(S\right)$ *Realization →* **#1 challenges** *#2*

#1:   My God. I mean, before, you know, you could prepare—you could set a place on the table inside yourself, so to say. You knew that, every Tuesday at two—

              $\left(S\right)$ *New tactic →* **#2 sympathizes** *w/ #1*

#2:   Or Friday at four, that was my—

#1:   You would be made to walk through the maze, and then be tied down upon a table—

#2:   Or in a chair, take your choice—

#1:   Hooked up—

#2:   Attached, exactly—

#1:   —to a machine, and made to look at yourself in the mirror while you were shot through with thousands of volts of electricity—

#2:   —which lasted just long enough for your body to start to burn—

                  $\boxed{K}$ **tempo** *relaxes after "yes"*

#1:   —for the smoke from your skin to start to—yes, that was the buzzer, that was the bell—

#2:   —that meant you could then weave your way back through the maze—

#1:   —if you could—or simply crawl—

#2:   —see, I could go home, that was why the Friday.

Subunit C: "The pattern was . . . healthy"
Rhythm: *regular, slow completion of #1's thought by #2; changes in actions are subtle, in the aftermath of the key moment*
Tempo: *calm, back to norm established in Subunit A*

(S) *Reaction* → *#1* **calms** *#2*

#1:   Fine. And it was accepted. On Tuesday, I knew I would take two sharp rights, go through a small swinging door, and experience eye-popping pain. The pattern was—

(S) *New tactic* → *#2* **seduces** *#1*

#2:   Healthy.

#1:   In the end, yes, that's what was proved, according to the experts.

Script Analysis

Following is a checklist for script analysis, with sample statements for *The New Rules* included beneath each item. Please see Chapter 2 for dramaturgical background.

1. **Core Action.** A succinct one- to three-sentence statement of the thrust of your interpretation that embraces all elements of production, plus an expanded one- to two-page version that suggests directions the ensemble might take.

    The New Rules *is about how two people scare each other to death (in one case, figuratively; in the other case, literally), fueled by their anxieties about unrealized threats. The key moment is when the rat-supervisors are heard, because this raises the level of anxiety beyond #2's threshold, in reaction to which his heart fails. The setting is a completely neutral and sterile space. It is a test space for humans, but the audience should realize this gradually, therefore the space should be disguised as something recognizable, but generic: a combination of a doctor's waiting room and no-man's-land.*

2. **Structure.** Is the play predominately climactic or episodic? How does the playwright structure time and events?

    The New Rules *is a short one-act play in one setting, with two characters. The only other presence is a group of rat-experimenters, unseen but heard at the key moment. It is climactic and time is continuous, although there is no definitive sense of when the action occurs, or how much time has passed prior to the play. It is almost as if the action exists in a time vacuum.*

3. **Unit Breakdown.** Divide the play up into the major units of action.

    See sample unit analysis above.

    Unit Titles

    - Find starting points for **actions/objectives** for each character.
    - Mark major **shifts** in actions and **key moments** in the margins.
    - Mark major **tempo** and **rhythm** shifts.
    - Trace the overall **arc** of each scene or the play and the **transitions** between scenes.

4. **Character.** *See sample unit analysis above.*
   - **Character traits:** What makes each character unique?
   - **Status:** What is each character's status like overall?
   - **Relationships:** How does each character relate to the others?
5. **Language.** What does the language reveal about the characters and their world?

   In The New Rules, *the characters are both articulate and sound educated. #2's anxiety is reflected in his more staccato use of language. There is little indication from the characters' use of language as to who they are or what they do, beyond the sense that this is their job. #2 refers to himself as "an accountant for a king," but there is no evidence corroborating this.*
6. **Groundplan.** Sketch a playable space within which the action of the play will take place.

   Virtually any empty space could be used. All that is required are a few chairs and possibly a couch to indicate a waiting room and give the actors obstacles to work around and a variety of configurations for them to interact within.
7. **Sound.** Note any required or selected environmental sounds or underscoring. What music will you use pre- and post-show? How will you handle transitions between scenes, if there are any? How does sound contribute to the core action?

   The only required sound in the play occurs when the audience and characters hear the scurrying of rats. This is the key moment of the play, since it causes #2's death, and therefore it should be frightening.
8. **Environment and Style.** What is the overall world of the play like? What values dominate the world?

   The world of The New Rules *is deliberately undefined, for the most part. The emphasis is on routine and obedience. Fear is the primary quality encouraged and valued by the unseen rats; #1's independence is a play for respect, though it only increases #2's fear of retribution.*

Dramaturgy Checklist

The following is a list of areas of inquiry that the director or dramaturg should explore as background research for preparing to direct a play. This list outlines the dramaturg's protocol, as advanced by Yale University's School of Drama. Depending upon your timetable, the type of play, and your resources, you may go into greater or lesser detail in any or all of these areas.

1. **Playwright's biography.** Focus on significant events that help you understand the concerns of the playwright. A playwright's life experiences may shape his or her playwriting in terms of subject matter, conflict, and character. But use this information carefully, as ultimately the text itself is more

important than anything you discover from outside the play. The play-wright's biography should inform your production, not dictate it.

2. **The writing of the play.** Are there other versions of the play in existence or any information available about how the play was written or developed? Earlier drafts or alternative versions of the play can help you understand why the playwright made certain choices in the final version. If you are directing a play that was originally written in another language, you should also search for any and all translations, as they will differ greatly depending upon when and where the play was translated. Translations are essentially different versions of the script, since translation is an art, not a science. Translators make choices about words, phrases, and ultimately even meaning. The tempos and rhythms of a play will differ depending upon how the play reads in a different language.

3. **History of past productions.** How has the play been produced and what does this tell you about the range of interpretation available? What hasn't been tried? What has been tried but failed? A play's production history should help you see the text as open to more than one interpretation, and stimulate your imagination to come up with alternatives to what other directors have done in the past.

4. **Other works by the playwright.** Reading other plays and writings by the playwright can give you a sense of his or her overall concerns, the place of this play within the playwright's overall works, and recurring structures, relationships, and actions. A playwright's body of work frequently reveals a pattern or evolution in his or her writing. Ibsen's plays, for example, fall into three distinct periods: his early historical plays, often in verse; his mid-career realistic plays; and his late symbolic plays. Understanding where a play fits within the playwright's career or how it prefigures or expands upon issues or characters in other plays will help you understand how your play functions.

5. **Historical, cultural, political, and religious background for the play.** From background research, you can gain a better understanding of the events of the play within their original historical context, as well as how the events might relate to what was happening in the playwright's world at the time he or she wrote the play.

6. **Criticism of the play.** Be selective in examining scholarly criticism of the play, as scholars do not always write with production concerns in mind; their interpretations can be skewed by the theories in vogue in their day. The script is always the test of any idea. Avoid heavily theoretical or unsubstantiated theories. Criticism is best thought of as a stimulant for your thoughts rather than a substitute for them.

5 Design Collaboration

In your early work as a director, in most cases your ensemble will consist primarily of actors. If you are very fortunate, you may have a stage manager in rehearsal, and he or she may run the show in production or work with an assistant stage manager or a light and/or sound board operator to implement some basic lighting or sound cues. Generally, though, you won't have a design team; instead, you'll design the production to the best of your abilities within an extremely limited budget. You might run sound cues from a portable CD player or computer. In these first productions, you will be directing and producing "poor theater." The term "poor" describes the financial and technical resources available to you, and is not meant to reflect the quality of the work.

As I stated in Chapter 3, poor theater has a long and illustrious history, beginning at least as far back as the earliest Greek drama, which occurred in the marketplace ("agora"), and reaching its heyday in the times of Shakespeare. The Elizabethan public theaters, such as Shakespeare's Globe, performed with a bare minimum of design support out of financial and artistic necessity. The companies performed a body of plays in repertory, with a different play every night, so as to attract a returning audience; each company might expect to perform over a hundred plays in a given season. Because of this, each company used stock costumes repeatedly. Rather than require unique scenery for each production, the Elizabethan playwrights wrote descriptions of the locations into their plays, so that the characters described the settings to the audience. This kept production costs low. In the Elizabethan era, elaborate spectacle could be found in the court masques, which were supported by royalty, but most productions during the period were performed as poor theater. Records indicate the plays did not suffer as a result, but flourished. Playwrights and companies did their best to overcome these limitations by being more creative with what they had. This is precisely the challenge that poor theatre presents; working on how to overcome the limitations of a low budget and minimal technical support will increase your ability to find creative solutions to the problems of bringing a whole dramatic world to the stage.

One of the keys in this level of production is to work creatively within the limitations of your budget, staff, and venue. You can produce compelling work without a fully equipped theater or even a permanent theater space; don't allow yourself to be limited by the notion that theater requires all of the trappings of a full production and a theater.

As you direct more productions, you may have the opportunity to work with greater resources and support, whether through an advanced directing class, an independent study, a community or local professional theater, or as part of the regular season of your theater department. If you have the chance to do so, you will quickly find yourself collaborating with many types of theater artists with whom you have not worked before, such as designers, playwrights, dramaturgs, and technical staff. The collaborative skills you have developed will help you with this future work, but each collaborative relationship brings specific challenges. In this chapter, we will focus on the director's relationship with designers.

As with any collaboration, the director/designer relationship will vary depending upon the individuals involved. Directors and designers collaborate in different ways depending upon the play, and the production circumstances and timetable. You will find that some designers enter the design process with strong ideas of their own, while others prefer to see where initial discussions with the director and other designers lead. Unless I have worked with the designers in the past, I usually begin the design process by talking with the design team about how I like to work and asking them how they like to work and what types of information help them most. This initial dialogue establishes the ground rules for the collaboration, by beginning to express each person's expectations. As the director, your first goal in collaborating with the design team is to get everyone on the same page and clarify what each person's responsibilities will be.

In some production situations, you may meet with one designer first, and then the other designers will join the process as you proceed. Under these circumstances, the set designer usually will be the first person you work with, followed by the costume designer, and then the lighting designer. The sound designer, if you have one, may come into the process at any time. This order of designers is based purely on practical concerns. The set designer often begins the process of creating the world of the play. The costume designer begins to create the characters within that world, staying sensitive to the set designer's color palate, which is often a joint decision of the director, the set designer, the costume designer, and the lighting designer, if possible. Including the costume designer in discussions about color helps the process greatly, as many plays require period-specific clothing using particular color palates. There is little sense in having the set designer begin to use particular colors if those colors will not complement the colors of the costumes. For this reason, discussing colors with your costume designer at an early stage may make your design process much more efficient, even if the costume designer is unable to fully participate in the early design meetings.

The lighting designer often enters the process last because he or she cannot draw up the **light plot**—a blueprint that indicates the types of lighting instruments to be used, where each lighting instrument will be hung, what color gel will go on it, and what area of the stage it will cover—until the set design has been finalized, since the location of the large stage properties and the walls, if any, will greatly influence the lighting designer's choices. If your production circumstances permit it, though, I recommend bringing all the designers into the design process from the start, as this creates the greatest sense of shared ownership of the production. It also tends to produce the most productive collaborations. Yet the staggered entry of designers into the process remains a common practice that you may encounter early in your directing, and therefore you should be prepared to address it in a collaborative way. One of the ways in which I have handled this situation is to include the entire design team in my initial design discussions via e-mail. In this way, the overall design can be addressed before one designer has proceeded too far in a particular direction, and all the designers can contribute and feel a part of the central decisions about the production.

If you are able to bring all the designers together for the first design meeting, design responsibilities will be shared somewhat differently. The set, costume, and lighting designers may all be involved in discussions and decisions about the overall world of the play, the stage configuration, the way in which the space will be used, the color palate, the period or style of the production, and the interaction among design elements. If you have a sound designer, he or she may raise issues about speaker placement, so that sound can come from particular places in the space at specific times. Speakers can even be incorporated into the set design, either visibly or hidden in the walls of the set, if the set designer is aware of this need early in the process.

It's generally better to have all the designers at the first design meeting so they can start out as equals in developing the production. As the director, you can then present your core action, discuss the shape of the action with your designers, and start to brainstorm with your design team. This provides the designers and director with the opportunity to create synergy: a blend of efforts and ideas that is greater than the sum of its parts. If you are specific about the action and raise questions as to how it can be achieved most effectively on stage, the designers will usually devise better solutions than you may have thought up on your own, because they will normally possess more design tools than you do.

A Designer Collaborates

I love working with directors who come to the first design meeting without a solution. They bring a passion for the play and might arrive with dozens of images that "feel" right, but without having made any final decisions as to how to tell the story. Such directors aren't unprepared; they are genuinely open. My favorite directors know the challenges and problems the script presents. For example, at the start of a production of *Macbeth*, one director told the designers, "This is a play about the psychology of Mac. The challenge is to make the internal external somehow, and to create a world in which the supernatural is a credible and essential element. I want to make it clear that Mac's problem is still relevant." Nothing in this statement dictates or even predicts a particular design answer. The director was not wed to period clothes. Presenting the challenge—"to externalize Macbeth's internal struggle"—opened up a series of lively discussions among the director and designers. The director did not tell us what to do or how to do it. The designers and director discovered an approach *together*.

Catherine Norgren has designed costumes for the Actors Theater of Louisville, Alabama Shakespeare Festival, Virginia Stage Company, Vermont Stage Company, and the Pennsylvania Stage Company.

By holding the design team true to your concept of the core action, you can achieve your vision while encouraging the best work in your designers. Review the pitches and outcomes below. You'll see that the statements of core action remain open to many visual interpretations, and the designers in each production discovered ways to achieve the director's vision that were not initially evident or inevitable. But can you imagine the pitches for these productions stimulating different designs?

Core Action Statements

In Chapter 2, we discussed the idea of core action as the guiding principle for using all of the directing elements in Chapter 4. Now that you have explored many of these elements, it's time to return to the core action and examine how a director might work with designers toward a realized vision of the action. Let's begin with the core action statement. The director should be able to explain the core action clearly, inspire the total ensemble to help flesh it out and give it shape, and choose wisely from among the ideas generated by the ensemble. As a director, you will regularly explain your core action orally and in writing, in such a way that it simultaneously inspires the ensemble to move out from this core and yet keeps them on track toward a coherent whole. You will need at least two versions of the core action: a condensed, one-paragraph version like you worked on in Chapter 2, and an expanded, more detailed one- to two-page version that suggests how your idea might be further explored by the ensemble. In this chapter, we'll be looking at the expanded version. Eventually, you might use the core action statement in any of the following settings:

- To propose a play to a theater or producer
- To start the process with designers
- To start the rehearsal process
- To generate excitement about the production in publicity and interviews

The final, one-paragraph statement of core action is the seed of your production, which can then be developed into the expanded statement (or vice versa, if you prefer). If you compare the final written statements of different directors working on the same play, you will probably find some strong similarities and some major differences as well. With a play such as *Betrayal*, which I choose deliberately for its ambiguities, a range of interpretations should be expected. Such differences are not a matter of right and wrong, but an expression of each director's individuality and creativity. Each interpretation will emphasize some elements of the play at the expense of others. You might have a particular gift for expressing your ideas succinctly and powerfully, but another director might take greater risks. Rather than competing with one another, discover what you can learn from one another. All great directors are influenced by a myriad of experiences, both personal and artistic. Learning from the other people in your class sets the groundwork for productive collaboration and a lifetime of learning from what others do and say.

From the seed of this one-paragraph statement, you should be able to expand the statement to include ideas about character choices, acting style, space, sound, setting, and other elements of production. If you are directing a "poor theater" production—one with no technical or design support, as will be the case for most of you in your first productions—the expanded pitch will help feed your actors' imaginations about the world of the play. When you have the luxury of a full team of designers and build crews, the complete pitch will begin the director–designer collaboration, which will lead to design sketches and models. In either case, making specific and clear choices that leave room for others to contribute usually leads to the strongest process and final product.

The final statement varies depending upon the type of play, the producer, and the circumstances of the play's production. If you are working with designers, you will usually write the first version of the core action statement with them in mind, and then you might read these first notes to the cast at the first rehearsal and read-through, before the designers show the cast the models and sketches for the production. In this way, the cast can see the original starting point for the process and the subsequent development of the production. It allows them to join into the production process and helps them understand how the collaboration started and developed. In most cases, the core action of the production will remain essentially the same from those initial notes, but the cast will be able to clearly see what the designers have contributed and how they have influenced and shaped the production. Choices about setting, character, and style will inform the future choices the actors will make. By presenting your ideas as a director first, you can assert your leadership over the production and process. The first presentation should stimulate the actors' imaginations and get them excited about the production, while motivating them to explore choices within the core action (as defined by the director) and the world of the play (as created by the designers).

You should consider starting your expanded statement by clarifying how you work and what you expect from your ensemble; for example, "My thinking about the play has begun to take shape, though I remain open as to how this vision is realized in terms of design elements. The starting point for every production for me is the action—defining it and then shaping it—and so I'd like to start off by talking about what I see in this play so far." The four sample pitches below cover a representative sample of theatrical genres (realism, avant-garde, verse, and Brechtian), time periods (Elizabethan, early modern, 1950s, and contemporary), and stage configurations (proscenium, black box, thrust, and arena). Each statement was sent or handed to the design team for that production first, and then read to the actors at the first cast meeting after the designs were well under way. Following each statement, you'll find a brief summary of how the design process evolved and some illustrations.

Hedda Gabler by Henrik Ibsen

I see *Hedda* as a play about the constructive and destructive sides of creativity. The character of Hedda is frequently maligned in theater criticism as lacking creativity or as merely being bored. I think that's a weak choice. I prefer to see Hedda as a rather brilliant woman who has been unable to find an outlet for her creativity in her world because she is a woman. So she ends up expressing her creativity in a negative way: by trying to destroy Løvborg in the "perfect suicide," a single bullet to the head (a destructive notion that Ibsen probably drew from the Romantics of the nineteenth century, but we also find it in destructive rock music lifestyles such as those of Janis Joplin, the punks, and grunge rock). I would like the cast to search for the contemporary rawness under the surface period-civility of the play, but beyond that I'm not sure at this time about setting and period, except to say that all the characters need to remain true to the text, and the costumes, regardless of period, need to reflect those characters.

I see the action as a chess game between two worthy foes, the protagonist and antagonist of the play: Hedda and Brack. This game is played out mostly through other people, including Løvborg, Madamoiselle Diana (through offstage action), and Thea; through the financial dealings that Brack employs prior to the start of the action of the play to set a trap for Hedda; and through Løvborg's manuscript (his and Thea's "baby") and Hedda's pistols. In the end, Brack comes to the edge of victory, which would allow him to "keep" Hedda as his mistress, only to find her willing to commit suicide to avoid this fate. In the end, she must create her own perfect suicide (a shot to the head) to wipe out the memory of Løvborg's botched suicide, which results instead in Madamoiselle Diana shooting him or Løvborg shooting himself accidentally, depending upon your reading of Brack's comments about this offstage action.

In this world, Thea is actually braver than Hedda, as she's willing to break society's rules and leave her husband, whereas Tesman is the ultimate conventional man. Unable as a scholar to be forward thinking and creative like Løvborg, he is only capable of cataloging old papers or reassembling the work of great thinkers like Løvborg posthumously. Aunt Julie shows us what happens to a woman without a baby in this world, reduced as she is to taking care of an invalid and nearly drooling over the possibility of taking care of Tesman and Hedda's baby. (By the way, I think it's fairly well established that Hedda is pregnant, if only implied by Ibsen due to the mores of the day, which prevented him from ever completing the characters' sentences that suggest pregnancy.) Brack shows the older man's place in this world—unlike Julie or Hedda, he can be respectable during the day and a free spirit, attending "orgies" at night. Women must either be seen in the day like Hedda, Thea, and Julie, or become "women of the evening" like Mademoiselle Diana.

Given this world, Hedda's choice to try to create Løvborg's perfect suicide serves as a sort of "suicide bomb" thrown into the psyche of this world. The pathetic thing is that when Hedda herself commits suicide in this matter, no one understands why she does it or why she might consider it a significant or even creative act. Thus all that Brack can say is "People don't do things like that." Hedda's final act of suicide is futile; beautiful only in her own eyes.

The acting style should focus on relationships, status, and the characters' manipulation of one another. It should be highly charged with emotion underneath a layer of civility and decorum. The characters barely hide their sexuality and aggression under a layer of superficiality, domesticity, and intellectuality.

I think we're looking for a set that is somewhat symbolic and abstract; simplicity is a key. The configuration could be thrust, arena, or environmental, so long as we keep an eye on the practical considerations of staging, such as entrances and exits, the drawing room that is Hedda's space, her piano, and her suicide. I believe the play has an autumnal mood to it, suggested to me by the earliest references to dying flowers, the death of the invalid aunt, and the eventual deaths of Løvborg, Hedda, and her fetus with her.

Design Process

As we worked together, my set designer suggested three stage configurations. In the one we both liked best, the play was performed in the round, with a ramp through the audience to the drawing room. I liked trying something new with this classic early modern play, written and traditionally performed on a proscenium stage. The setting and costumes stayed loosely period, though simplified and somewhat symbolic (see Figure 5.1).

The last piece in the design puzzle was the backdrop for Hedda's drawing room, which extended an autumnal pattern of roots from the floor to a scrim stretched on an oversized picture frame, so that Hedda's final suicide could be staged within the frame, like a work of art revealed through the scrim after the last line of the play. A sixty-second light cue, accompanied by operatic music and culminating in the lights slowly fading out, gradually built the final image so that it lingered in the audience's minds like an afterimage (see Figure 5.2).

FIGURE 5.1   *Hedda Gabler.* Overall view of stage. Scene Design: Tim
Golebiewski.

FIGURE 5.2   *Hedda Gabler.* The final image of the production:
Hedda's suicide framed by the thick wooden borders of her parlor,
revealed through a scrim. Hedda: Kristin Knapp.

The Baltimore Waltz by Paula Vogel

The central action of the play is Anna's imaginary journey through Europe to an imaginary cure for her disease in Vienna. The play begins with Anna asking for help. Her line "Help me please" is, I think, a genuine plea for help that she then covers up by translating it into Dutch a moment later. At the climax of the play the key line is the Third Man's "Wo ist dein Bruder?" (Where is your brother?). For me this sums up her journey: As Anna travels further and further from Baltimore in her mind, searching for help by trying to put herself in Carl's place (taking on a mock version of his disease, sleeping with men), she forgets her brother. Only in the conclusion of the play, after we discover that Carl has died, does Anna truly embrace his death and his life in the final "waltz" of the title.

The play is episodic, with sharp breaks in action, punctuated by Brechtian direct address "lessons" and style shifts. As a second-generation AIDS play—a black comedy—the action centers more on coping with dying than on the disease itself. Many of the Third Man's characters are taken from Hollywood films and popular culture. Vogel's method of appropriating and parodying old films is a key to the shape of the play and the production. Look at the films *The Third Man* and *Dr. Strangelove* for possible clues to the visual style. The Ferris wheel scene is based on a scene from *The Third Man* and I think that the significance of Anna's name comes from this movie as well, just as the dueling hands of Dr. Todesrocheln (German for "death rattle") come from *Dr. Strangelove*. Let's also look at the other films that Vogel mentions, though these appear to be less central.

At the top of the play, Vogel notes that the setting is a hospital lounge in Baltimore. I like the idea of taking her direction quite literally and making everything on stage something we might find in the hospital lounge or hospital. Much as Anna tries to escape from the hospital, she's always there. It's as if the whole play is a dream made up of Hollywood images of Europe constructed from materials taken from the Baltimore hospital, or as if this is a game that Anna and Carl play together in the hospital as they approach his death.

The space needs to be flexible and fluid to accommodate the numerous transitions between scenes seamlessly. Let's consider using one or two actor-stagehands dressed as hospital attendants to help with the scene changes and reinforce the feeling that we've never left the hospital.

We need something on which to project Carl and Anna's "travel slides." Can we find something from the hospital environment that could be used for slide projection and perhaps also be worked into the scenes in another way? As for the slides themselves, I'm hoping we can rent most of them from a previous production and just shoot the two or three that are supposed to include Anna.

Design Process

The set designer for this production was a professional designer with extensive experience who was accustomed to rendering a fairly complete set design before talking to the director for this particular venue. After we spoke, we adapted our working style to each other. We realized that our initial interpretations were vastly different: He saw the play as pure fantasy, whereas I wanted it to be fantasy grounded in the reality of the space (a hospital) where Anna stays with her brother. In this case, I considered the alternative interpretation, but ultimately rejected it as inconsistent with my core action. The designer then came up with many imaginative ways to use elements of an actual hospital to create Anna's fantasy. Most of the settings were created from four waiting room benches on wheels, which were reconfigured for each scene by two "hospital attendants"— nonspeaking parts in hospital garb. When Anna imagines herself dining with Carl in Paris, the two dine on Jell-O™ instead of French cuisine. When they ride the train, the two hospital attendants become coat racks and create the sound effects, and the rocking motion of the actors suggests a train in motion. For one of the hotel room scenes, the two attendants hold lamp shades in front of their faces to simulate a "cinematic" top view of the scene (see Figure 5.3). And the Third Man's clandestine visit to threaten Anna transforms the hospital setting through the use of film noir lighting effects (see Figure 5.4).

FIGURE 5.3 *The Baltimore Waltz.* The hospital attendants hold a sheet and two lamp shades to create a "cinematic" top view of the scene. Carl: Daniel Leary. Anna: Gina Gargone. Scene Design: Bob Phillips.

FIGURE 5.4 *The Baltimore Waltz.* When the Third Man threatens Anna, film noir lighting transforms the hospital into a dangerous space defined by shadows and steeply angled lighting.

The Birthday Party by Harold Pinter

On the most basic level, *The Birthday Party* is about a man who is afraid to leave the house. First Meg, then Lulu, and finally Goldberg and McCann try to stir Stanley to leave his room and then the house. Their tactics vary tremendously, from Meg and Lulu's flirtations to the black comedy and menace of Goldberg and McCann.

Act One establishes the safety and warmth of the house, Meg's odd maternal/sexual relationship with Stanley, Stanley's fear of Lulu (her name is a reference to Wedekind's Lulu, one of the most sexual female characters in all of dramatic literature), the threat of people invading this safe space, and the arrival of this threat in the form of Goldberg and McCann. Act Two is The Party, a carnivalesque, at times surreal attack on Stanley's sanity. Act Three maintains our interest primarily through Stanley's absence. We wonder "Where Is Stanley?" only to find that the answer Pinter offers at the end of the play remains utterly ambiguous. Ambiguity is one of the keys to the play for me. Let's try to resist concrete answers to the questions, such as "Who are Goldberg and McCann?" "What has Stanley done?" "Where are they taking him?"

I see a lot of vaudeville in Goldberg and McCann. Their rapid-fire questions in Act Two ("Why did the chicken cross the road? Which came first, the chicken or the egg?") remind me of Abbott and Costello or Laurel and Hardy, and their names may indicate stock Jewish and Irish comedians from vaudeville. Petey and Meg, on the other hand, seem like stock characters from a mystery or thriller, their everyday existence about to be toppled by the strange visitors Goldberg and McCann. I'd like to see how far we can take this. Let's look for the vaudeville moments that disrupt the safety of this house and find ways to disrupt the stock realism established at the beginning of Act 1 with the theatricality of vaudeville—song and dance, wild costumes that transform instantly, cross-fire comedic timing, magic, ragtime piano music.

Design Process

In this production, the designers were all graduate design students. The set designer worked within a "palette" of discarded objects, building the set from items that could have been discarded as Stanley has been discarded, a suggestion I made early on with which he connected. The costume and lighting designers embraced the vaudeville elements fully, researching and incorporating stock vaudeville conventions into the set, and creating a carnivalesque birthday party, as when the formerly innocent Lulu dresses up as a showgirl to flirt with Goldberg (see Figure 5.5).

FIGURE 5.5 *The Birthday Party.* In this scene, Lulu flirtatiously stretches herself across the table and Goldberg responds but maintains his high status, while Meg remains a distant spectator. Costume design: Shauna Meador. Lulu: Jill Robinson. Meg: Julie Willis. Goldberg: Andrew Persinger.

Twelfth Night by William Shakespeare

I've cut the play by about 20 percent, and all cuts occur *within* scenes. I have at-tached a copy of the cut script. Since the cuts keep the major lines of action in-tact, they should not have a major effect on our work. They are meant to streamline the action, not alter it.

One thing that I noticed immediately about the script is that by our stan-dards, most of the couplings at the end of the play seem almost arbitrary, aside from perhaps Viola-Orsino. After all, Olivia and Sebastian barely know each other, and Toby and Maria seems a hasty, if somehow appropriate, pairing. But I was struck by two lines in particular, each of which occurs at the very end of an act:

> Olivia (I, v): Fate, show thy force; ourselves we do not owe;
> What is decreed must be, and be this so.

> Viola (III, iv): O! if it prove,
> Tempests are kind, and salt waves fresh in love.

The sense I get from the action of the play, captured by these two lines, is that love is fate: a force of nature. I also noticed that the characters talk about "the elements" a lot, which in Shakespeare's day would be earth, water, fire, and air. And that it's a storm that brings all these lovers together.

This is my starting point, right now—a world that's elemental, natural, forceful, fateful. I think it's a world full of pleasures that few are able to taste until the end of the play, with the exception of Toby, who is subject to scorn and re-bukes for overindulging. Nature rules, and only nature will break what has be-come an unnatural mourning process for Olivia (who mourns her brother and father and intends to do so for seven years!) and Sebastian and Viola (who believe they are in mourning for each other). And conversely Malvolio is teased and tor-mented by the overindulgers, Toby and Maria, for rejecting pleasure and nature.

I am most intrigued by a contemporary setting, but I'm open to other ideas. In Shakespeare's day, they performed almost all plays, except those in Greek or Roman settings, in what was contemporary dress for them. I'd like to do the same. I'm not particularly interested in a trendy time-shift to another era. And if it's contemporary, I'd like to keep it simple. I'm intrigued by the notion of find-ing a contemporary equivalent for the Elizabethan stage, but one not bound by the specific conventions of that stage. Something simple that allows us to move through transitions with ease, grace, and speed. Illyria, in Shakespeare's day, was a resort area by the sea, so this might be a beach resort, though I'd rather we sug-gest that. I don't see a realistic Club Med on stage! But textures such as sand, water, rocks, dunes, all feel right for this play.

I am open to any stage configuration, although I am least interested in proscenium. I lean toward a deep thrust, arena, or environmental setting. I'd like to find a way to surround the audience with this world and make them feel a part of it. I lean toward a simple setting, but I'm flexible. Over 50 percent of the scenes and 80 percent of the lines occur at or near Olivia's house, but half the play is set outdoors. As the play progresses, the scenes tend to move outdoors more and more, almost as if the figurative "storm" of Viola's and Sebastian's arrival has forced everyone outside, to confront nature. It seems to me, though, that almost all of the scenes could be played outdoors, with the possible exception of II, iii, the drinking scene, which at least needs to be close enough to Olivia's house to disturb Malvolio and Olivia.

I do have some specific staging ideas I'm playing around with and thought I should mention. First, in keeping with the idea of "love as a force of nature," I'd like to stage the storm between I, i and I, ii, as a sort of movement piece set to music. What do you think? And I might like to suggest in some way that the climax of the play is like a storm, too, though I'm not sure yet how we'd do this.

The low comic characters are mostly social climbers and parasites, whereas the romantics are more affluent; therefore they overly idealize love because it's the only thing in life that they lack. I should warn you that since we have a large number of actresses and very few actors in the department right now, I will probably change several supporting roles (including Feste and Fabian) to female. I do not see these changes as conceptual, but they will affect the production, if only on a practical level. Each character would find a simple contemporary equivalent. Perhaps the most radical idea I'm playing with is for Feste to be the island drug dealer, singing Bob Marley songs to earn her keep. This is in keeping with the Elizabethan theater's use of songs that its patrons would immediately recognize.

Some questions to keep in the back of our minds: How is Malvolio imprisoned? Do we see him or just hear him? Is he in a straitjacket, or blindfolded, or buried in a hole in the ground? How/where do Toby, Andrew, and Fabian hide to watch Malvolio in the letter scene?

Design Process

The final design found the simplicity I sought within a contemporary setting. Olivia's bedroom was rendered in forced perspective (an idea that the set designer and I arrived at together) and became a tiny, cryptic room that later became Malvolio's dungeon, so that he is imprisoned in the very place he most desires (see Figure 5.6). The actor playing Malvolio suggested that the contemporary version of "yellow stockings, cross-gartered" would be for his character to be a cross-dresser, a hilarious choice that the costume designer went along with after some debate (see Figure 5.7).

DISCUSSION QUESTIONS

In small groups of two to four, discuss some of the following questions as they apply to the statements above, your scene statements, or the statements for your one-act plays. You might also redo the core action exercise in Chapter 2, and discuss your results. Try to reach a consensus on the

FIGURE 5.6   *Twelfth Night.* Olivia's miniature house becomes Malvolio's prison, confining him to the very place he most desires. Malvolio: Luke Rosen. Scene Design: Takeshi Kata. Lighting Design: Matthew Richards.

most important aspects of the group's answer to each question. When each group has reached a consensus or a deadlock, reassemble as a large group to share and discuss the answers.

1. What is the most compelling sentence of the statement and why?

2. Does the statement inspire design and acting choices? In what directions do you see these choices going?

3. Is the statement clear and specific, yet open to further development by the individual designers and actors? What responsibilities remain for the other ensemble members?

4. Does the statement describe an arc through the play or production? Does it appear likely to drive the production?

EXERCISE

If you don't have designers available for this exercise, you can each serve as designers for the purpose of learning about design collaboration. Break down into groups of three to four; one of you will take the role of the director, while the others will take the role of designers. Using one of the

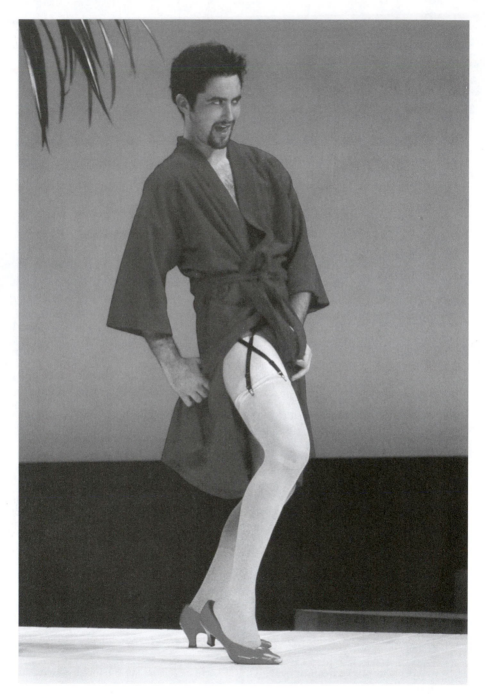

FIGURE 5.7 *Twelfth Night.* Malvolio's "yellow stockings" revealed his secret desire to cross-dress. Malvolio: Luke Rosen. Costume Design: Herta Payson.

statements from the previous section, read the play and meet as a group outside of class to discuss it. The director may use the existing pitch or alter it in any way he or she sees fit; this can be the director's decision or a group decision at the director's discretion. Having settled upon a core action, the "director" and "designers" then do visual research in art and photography books and magazines for images that might be the basis for a design based upon the core action. Meet again and compare your imagery. Working as a team, select or combine images to produce a new vision of the play for the production.

Discussion

1. As a team, present your new pitch and images to the class. Discuss the ramifications of your choices and get feedback on whether the imagery successfully achieves the aims of the pitch.

2. Looking over the range of choices made by each group, discuss as a class the different approaches. Has each group succeeded in making the production their own? What were the dynamics of the collaborations?

Design Timetable

The process of working with designers will, as stated above, differ depending upon the production circumstances and theater company or venue with which you are working. Whether you begin working with your entire design team at the same time or start with one designer and add other designers into the process as you go, you should be aware of the basic structure of the design process, what you can expect the designer to provide you with at each phase, and what sort of feedback will work best at each stage of the process. If you do not have a production manager doing so already, set up a calendar that includes all due dates for designs, including preliminary designs and final designs, as well as the schedule for loading in the set and lights, adding in the costumes, and working through technical and dress rehearsals. Here's a brief outline of a "typical" design process. Keep in mind that different theaters and designers will deviate from this model greatly, so it is best to agree upon a process and a timetable with your designers and theater staff at the beginning of the process.

1. **Initial design meeting.** Director pitches his or her core action for the production, details all necessary design elements or challenges (such as trap doors, ways of making transitions between scenes, and so on). Designers ask questions to clarify the director's interpretation, offer alternative interpretations or changes, and/or begin to suggest different ways of realizing the director's interpretation from a designer's point of view. Some designers may prefer to do

additional research before pitching their own ideas; others may come to the initial design meeting with some ideas already in mind. I suggest sending a brief, one- or two-page statement of your intentions (see my sample pitches earlier in this chapter for examples) before the initial meeting, so that the designers come to the meeting with some idea of your intentions and perhaps some ideas of their own. The central goal of the initial design meeting is to advance your interpretation and begin to come to an agreement with the design team on a more refined version of this statement.

2. Brainstorming phase. During this phase, the designers will usually bring in visual imagery (or in the case of a sound designer, sounds and music) that captures the essence of one or more possible ways of achieving the agreed-upon core action.

- *Set designers* may bring in photographs, visual art, architecture, or even advertising images that reflect one or more overall approaches to the scene. They may share images that illustrate an aspect of the play, such as the period, the style, or the color palatte, or a series of images that take you through the progression of the play.
- *Lighting designers* may bring in photographs and visual art that display particular "lighting looks"—ways of using the direction, quality, color, and intensity of light from scene to scene.
- *Costume designers* may bring in photographs and visual research that display a range of possible approaches to the costumes in the production. They may show you visual research that captures their conception of particular characters.
- *Sound designers* may bring in music and sound effects that capture the world of the play, or particular ideas they may have about an overall sound motif for the production.
- *The director's response.* As director, you need to give honest feedback on what works for you as early as possible. Although you should remain open to your designers' ideas, don't encourage them to proceed with an approach that you don't feel comfortable with simply to appear collaborative. As the director, you must respect not only the ideas of your designers, but also their time and energy. Encourage them to explore the ideas that you like the best; tell them as early as possible when you have serious reservations. When the design team and director have agreed upon a basic direction for the production design, you are ready to move on to the next phase.

3. Rendering and model phase. Once the design team and director have agreed upon a basic approach to the design elements in production, each designer will begin to flesh out his or her design in more detail. Each design area uses a different set of tools to communicate the design to you and each other. They may use any or all of the following:

- *Set designers* May use **thumbnail sketches,** full-page black-and-white, color or computerized renderings (see Figures 5.8 and 5.9), **white**

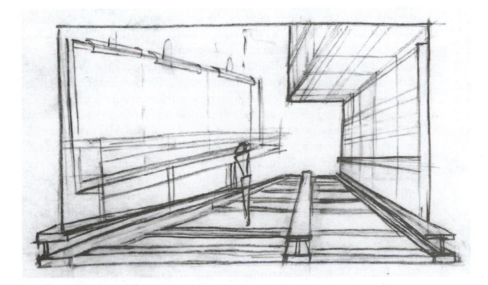

FIGURE 5.8 *Macbeth*. Scene Design: Lynne M. Koscelniak. A pencil rendering such as this one is usually one of the first steps in the design process.

FIGURE 5.9 *Macbeth*. Scene Design: Lynne M. Koscelniak. Computer renderings such as this one allow the designer tremendous flexibility in experimenting with a design.

models (all-white scale models of the set, intended to show the use of space before all the designers agree upon a color palate), scale models of the design (see Figure 5.10) in full color and texture. Scale models are usually built in ¼- or ½-inch scale, which means that each ¼ or ½ inch of the model equals 1 foot on the actual stage. The set designer will need a complete set of plans for the theater to build an accurate model.

■ Many *lighting designers* continue to use photographs to communicate their design ideas. Most of those trained in BFA and MFA theater programs in the past two or three decades, however, will draw lighting sketches to reflect the **lighting looks** they have in mind, often working off of the renderings that the set designer has drawn. Eventually, they will draft a **light plot**: a blueprint of the stage from above that shows all the lighting positions, the lighting instruments the designer will place in each spot, the types of lighting instruments, and the direction and gel color for each one. Light plots are notoriously hard for directors to understand, unless they have considerable lighting experience themselves. Your designer should be willing and able to walk you through the light plot and explain, in broad terms, how it will work.

FIGURE 5.10 *Macbeth.* Scene Design: Lynne M. Koscelniak. A scale model has the added advantage of providing the director and ensemble with the sense of a space in three dimensions.

- Make sure that the set designer, sound designer, and technical director see the light plot as early as possible, since adjustments may need to be made to accommodate the requirements of all the designs. For example, the set designer may need to fly out a wall to make a transition between scenes; he or she will have to work with the lighting designer to make sure that this can be done safely and smoothly. Similarly, the sound designer may wish to place speakers above the stage, in which case he or she will need to work with the lighting and set designers to work out the best place for the speakers to achieve the sound design in coordination with the needs of the other design areas.

- In the **rendering** phase, the *costume designer* may show of you photographs or sketches of costumes he or she would like to buy, build, and/or pull from stock. Your designer may also show you **swatches** of material: small samples of fabric he or she intends to use. Look at everything the designer shows you very carefully. Make sure the costumes reflect your shared sense of the characters and the world that they inhabit. Think about combinations of characters that are essential to understanding the play, such as family members, friends, and arch enemies, as well as places and functions in which the characters will wear the costumes. Imagine the characters in these costumes performing the physical tasks of the play: Will they be able to do so? Again, examine the color palette of the production: Do the colors of all the designs complement each other? Be sure that there is enough contrast between each costume and the dominant colors in the set, so that the characters don't disappear into the environment.

4. Implementation phase. Once the design team and the director have agreed upon final designs, the scene shop and the costume shop will begin to buy materials, draw final plans, perhaps construct a **full-color model**, measure the actors in costume fittings, and construct designs. Visit the shops frequently—at least once a week—during this phase of the process. Visiting the shops shows your continued interest in the collaboration and in the work that goes in to realizing the designs. As long as you are friendly and do not appear to be second-guessing your designers, they should take your visits as signs of interest, not concern. Many times an early visit to the shop will allow you to pick up on an error in communication that you may have missed earlier.

5. Technical/dress rehearsals. Before you enter the space, consider having a **paper tech** with the stage manager, lighting designer, and sound designer, particularly if you are working with student designers and a student (or first-time) stage manager. A paper tech consists of the four of you sitting down, about a week before the technical rehearsal, and penciling in the rough cues for the production. It allows this group to coordinate their efforts, gives you all a sense of the combined rhythm of the production, gives your stage manager some time to enter most of the cues in the promptbook, and encourages you to make some basic decisions before you enter the theater, which in turn will speed the process once you enter the theater.

- The first thing you should know as you enter into your first true **technical rehearsal** is that every theater has its own system of handling tech. By and large, in the "old school" of tech, there will be a **cue-to-cue**, in which you will go through the production on a "stop-and-go" basis, stopping for every moment when where is a cue, setting it, and then skipping ahead to the next cue. This system is based upon the assumption that each cue will take some time to set up; this was indeed the case before computerized systems allowed designers and board operators to enter cues quickly, laying them over a run-through as it proceeds. Designers and technical directors who have worked in this system for years may still work this way; those who learned on computerized systems will prefer to skip the cue-to-cue. You may have a combination of approaches on your design team, so it's important to agree on whether you will be having a cue-to-cue before you move into the theater.

- In some theaters, you may be given time on stage to work with the actors before technical rehearsals. If your time on stage is limited, your technical rehearsals may be one of the first times your actors are on stage. You must adjust your goals to these circumstances.

- Either way, make it clear to your cast that you will have to devote much of your attention in technical rehearsals to the designers and technical staff. They need this time to support the work your ensemble has achieved in rehearsal. Your actors must know that your attention will be primarily focused on technical matters; they should be patient and try to be responsive to the needs of the designers and technical staff while adjusting to the demands of the real space.

- Technical rehearsals provide the cast with creative opportunities if they concentrate on what they can learn as everyone else is trying to figure out how the production works in this space. Encourage them to be sensitive to the space, look to see what adjustments they will have to make to the space, and experiment with how their voices fill the space.

- A *cue-to-cue* is still a valid way to set up cues for a show, particularly if you are using old light boards with no computers. But by and large you will save time in tech, and gain a sense of how the cues fit into the rhythm of the show, by laying in the cues over a run-through. The designers and technical staff can still call for a pause should they need time to work on a particular cue.

- *Dry tech* is often misunderstood. Should people use this term, ask what they do in a dry tech, and you'll get a better idea of what they mean. I was taught that a dry tech was a tech without actors, but I never saw the need or use for this when light cues can be changed so quickly on today's computerized light boards.

- Usually you will get two or three **technical rehearsals** or *tech runs*. The first one may involve a lot of stop and go, as your designers and technical staff may miss the moment for a cue, or want to try it again. During the second and third technical run, your actors will get to run scenes with little or no interruption, and you should be able to give them acting notes. I still recommend focusing on the technical aspects and adjusting the staging so that it fits the actual theater and does not create any sight line problems. During tech runs, move around the audience to see if most moments can be seen and heard from various parts of the theater.

- Not all theaters have a **costume parade**, but I recommend one if possible. The costume parade gives you the opportunity to sit down in the audience with the costume designer and see the costumes under the actual lighting, uninterrupted by other concerns. It is your last chance to truly examine the costumes and make any suggestions. I prefer to hold a costume parade before the first technical run (usually Monday for a Thursday opening), as it gives the actors a preview of their costumes, gives the designer adequate opportunity to fix any problems, and won't tire out your actors too close to opening.

- A **photo call** can be held during or after dress rehearsals. Some theaters have a photographer take shots during a dress rehearsal or a performance. I find this to be disturbing to the actors, and the shots usually don't turn out as well. A photo call allows you to predetermine what shots are most important to you. It should serve several purposes: (1) publicity shots for local newspapers; (2) portfolio shots for the director's and designers' portfolios; (3) archival shots for the theater or institution; (4) shots for the actors. Although with the proper film and filters it is possible to get excellent photographs on film, it is now cheaper and easier to take digital photographs. If possible, use a camera with at least 4.0 megapixels; this should be good enough to capture shots with good enough resolution to enlarge the photographs to 8 by 10 inches. Digital photography makes it easier for you to transfer the shots to a website (yours or the institution's), correct the colors, and crop the shots. Taking the shots during a photo call rather than a run-through or performance allows you to freeze the actors for crisper shots, boost the lighting from the booth if more light is needed, and change your camera angle and position. Most young directors today take their own production shots rather than relying upon their designers or the publicity office. The portfolio is a primary documentation of the director's work, and an important way of describing what you do as a director and how you've approached past productions.

- During the **dress rehearsals**, you will finally get to see the entire production, with all elements in place, hopefully without a stop. Forewarn your actors that stops may be necessary; better to fix something during a dress rehearsal than try to fix it afterward and worry if it will actually work. You will need to take notes on all aspects of production, from the performances to design to scene shifts. Come up with a code of letters or symbols that you can write in the margins so that you will be able to pick out the different types of notes. Following the run-through, you will in all likelihood meet separately with the designers and with the cast, and this will go more smoothly if you can isolate each group's notes. Be sure to have your stage manager keep an accurate running time on a stop watch, pausing for major interruptions, so that you have a good idea of how long the production is taking. By the last dress rehearsal, keep your acting notes short and to the point. It doesn't help to repeat a small note for the umpteenth time; go for the essentials or small notes that have the maximum effect on the shape of the production.

KEY TERMS

Lighting looks.   Sketches drawn by the lighting designer to communicate to the director and the other designers how the lighting should look in each scene or key moment. The sketches should reflect the direction and intensity of the lighting in the scene and give an overall sense of the mood. They may be based upon the set designer's renderings, or may be more figurative and thus less realistic.

Thumbnail sketches.   In the early stages of the design process, designers may draw rough sketches in miniature, slightly bigger than a postage stamp, to communicate their initial design ideas to the director and to one another.

White models.   When a set designer has moved beyond visual research, thumbnail sketches, and renderings, he or she may build a three-dimensional model of the set in $\frac{1}{4}$- or $\frac{1}{2}$-inch scale, constructed solely out of white cardboard or poster board. The purpose of such a model is to communicate a sense of the set's structural appearance before selecting the color palette for the entire production.

Full-color models.   In the final stages of the design process, the set designer will often create a full-color model in $\frac{1}{4}$- or $\frac{1}{2}$-inch scale. These models may be quite detailed and elaborate, and they are usually quite accurate in terms of color and texture. They serve as the final model for design team and director to examine before the set designer drafts the blueprints from which the technical director and staff will build the set.

Scale.   When a model is built to scale, this means that a unit or measurement of the model represents a larger unit on the actual set. One-quarter-inch scale means that every $\frac{1}{4}$ inch on the model equals 1 foot on the set; one-half-inch scale means that every $\frac{1}{2}$ inch on the model equals 1 foot on set. By measuring the model, we can figure out exactly how large something will be on a real set.

Light plot.   The lighting designer's blueprint indicating the position, direction, color, and type of each lighting instrument to be used in the production is called the light plot. From the light plot, the lighting designer should be able to tell the director and the design team how various parts of the stage will be lit during each scene. Computer programs allow lighting designers to previsualize light plots (see Figures 5.11 and 5.12).

Costume renderings.   The costume designer may draw black-and-white sketches or full-color renderings of most or all of the costumes in the production. The designer may use these renderings to communicate his or her ideas about each costume or group of costumes, as well as the progression of each character's costumes throughout the production.

Swatches.   To better communicate the colors, textures, and weight of the costumes, costume designers may show the design team and director swatches, which are small pieces of the actual fabrics the designer intends to use.

Paper tech.   Before moving the production into the theater for technical rehearsals, some production teams will hold a paper tech, usually attended by the director, the stage manager, the lighting designer, and the sound designer. This group will go through the production cue by cue, with the stage manager marking down these preliminary cues in his or her promptbook. This allows the director and designers to coordinate the cues to provide the stage manager with a better sense of how the show will be cued before the first technical rehearsal.

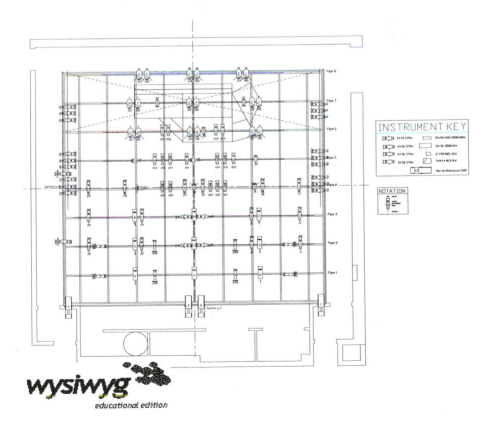

FIGURE 5.11   Computer programs such as wysiwyg allow lighting designers to draft a light plot and also visualize the lighting instruments in three dimensions in the theater space. Lighting Design: Bryan A. Kaczmarek.

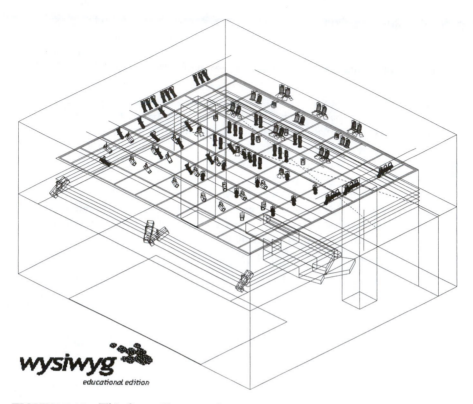

FIGURE 5.12   This figure illustrates the previous light plot in three dimensions. Lighting Design: Bryan A. Kaczmarek.

Cue-to-cue.   Before the advent of computerized light boards, the first technical rehearsal was normally a "cue-to-cue"—a rehearsal in which the ensemble jumped from one cue to the next, skipping the material in between. Some lighting designers still employ this method, although most prefer to create the cues during a run-through. Computerized light boards have made this much easier to do, and creating the cues as the actors perform allows the designers and technical staff to time the cues so that they blend with the action on stage.

Costume parade.   Some theater companies hold a costume parade, in which the actors come on stage in their costumes so that the director and costume designer can discuss changes and finishing touches. The costume parade is usually held a couple of days before the first dress rehearsal, to give the designer and director sufficient time to make any necessary changes. As the director, you can minimize the need for last-minute changes by attending the final fittings in the last couple of weeks of rehearsal.

Technical rehearsals.   Two or three rehearsals are devoted to technical rehearsals. During this time, the technical elements of the production will gradually be introduced, first the lighting cues and set, followed (or in concert with) the sound cues. The first tech rehearsal may be a dry tech or cue-to-cue (see above), or the production team may try to "lay in" the cues over a run-through of the play. The most important thing to remember (and to tell your cast) as you start the first technical rehearsal is that the director's attention must stay primarily on technical and design matters during tech. Actors should concentrate on accommodating themselves to the set, and beginning to learn how to fill the actual performance space, but they should not expect detailed notes from the director, although under some circumstances such notes may be possible. As long as the director makes this clear to the actors at the beginning of tech, and gives them suggestions as to what they can work on during this period, the tech rehearsals will be fruitful for everyone.

Dress rehearsals.   The last two or three rehearsals will be dress rehearsals; the very last rehearsal before opening might be used as an open or invited dress rehearsal, so that the cast starts to become used to the presence of an audience and how that may affect their performances. For example, audience laughter may change the rhythm of the production, either by forcing the actors to wait for laughter to subside, or through the adrenaline burst that the audience's attention and energy often gives the cast. At this point (if not before), costumes are added to the production, and all final touches on the set and adjustments to the lighting should become finalized. The director must juggle all his or her tasks at this point, including notes on acting, design, and the overall rhythm of the production that is created when all elements are brought together, including the cuing of the production by the stage manager, a major but often overlooked part of the rhythm of the production. This is the director's final chance before opening to solidify the structure, arc, and elements of production to achieve the core action that began as the director's vision. During the run of the production, the director may continue to give notes, but by the final dress rehearsal, the director should begin to let go of the production, and allow the ensemble to own it, power it, and continue to shape it and give it life.

SUPPLEMENTAL READING

Jones, Robert Edmund. *The Dramatic Imagination*. New York: Theatre Arts Books, 1941.

Kaye, Deena, and James Lebrecht. *Sound and Music for the Theatre: The Art and Technique of Design*. 2nd ed. Burlington, MA: Focal, 1999.

Pecktal, Lyn. *Costume Design: Techniques of Modern Masters*. New York: Watson-Guptill, 1999.

———. *Designing and Drawing for the Theater*. New York: McGraw-Hill, 1994.

———. *Designing and Painting for the Theatre*. New York: Holt, Rinehart and Winston, 1975.

Rosenthal, Jean, and Lael Wertenbaker. *The Magic of Light*. Boston: Little, Brown, 1972.

6 Other Collaborators

Playwrights

Collaborating with the playwright on a new play can be an extraordinary experience. When you work on a play with the playwright in residence, you have a unique opportunity to contribute to the shaping of the text, by making suggestions for revisions, trying out new paths, and providing the playwright with feedback throughout the revision process, which can even take place during the rehearsal period. Working on a new play also requires tremendous sensitivity because the playwright—as the creator of the dialogue, characters, and action— has the strongest personal connection to the material and may have fixed ideas about the play. Your collaboration starts with the recognition of the personal nature of the playwright's creation. Talk to the playwright at the start of your collaboration; come to an agreement early in the process as to how you are going to work together.

As the director of a new work you may enter the process at a variety of stages. Frequently, you will be involved in the early readings or workshops of the play. These provide the opportunity for you to help the playwright craft a better play. Your ability to collaborate with the playwright on a reading or workshop may lead to the opportunity to direct a full production of the play. Over the past four or five decades, this system of "play development" has become standard at most professional theaters that produce new plays. Many directors get their first professional directing work by successfully collaborating on a reading with a playwright; many playwrights value their relationships with particular directors so much that they depend upon these directors to direct all their work.

Readings and Staged Readings

There are two basic types of readings: **staged readings**, in which the actors move around the space with script in hand; and **readings**, in which the actors sit in a row or semicircle and read from the script. In either case, to maximize the usefulness of the reading to the playwright and the director, the actors should receive copies of the script at least twenty-four hours before the reading. This gives them time to highlight their lines, become comfortable with their roles, and make basic decisions about their characters' actions and objectives. Your responsibilities as a director will change depending upon the type of reading, and the objective and audience for the reading.

When directing a staged reading, before you go into the first rehearsal you should have some sense of how you will block the action, particularly at key moments and in large groups scenes. If, as is often the case, you have minimal rehearsal time, you should come into the first rehearsal with all the blocking written down. You can communicate a great deal about your interpretation of the play through this blocking, and by focusing in the actors' responsibilities on the text and their actions you will make the most of their contributions to the collaboration. You should also have a clear statement of the core action of the play: a brief statement that you can make to the actors at the beginning of the rehearsal period to focus them immediately on a shared vision or goal. Your statement of the core action can also serve to focus your discussions with the playwright before and after the reading.

Readings (seated) are usually given very little rehearsal time. You might only have time to read through the script once with the actors and give them notes; sometimes you won't even have time for a read-through. The goal is more limited: to hear the play, understand the action, and identify what additional work needs to be done on the text. Focus on the core action and encourage the actors to make strong choices about characters, actions, and overall objectives.

Workshop productions present a different set of challenges for the director, as you are aiming to show what a finished production of the play might look like on minimal resources. The play might have already gone through several readings and/or staged readings; therefore the script should be closer to final form. How much rehearsal time you have will determine how much you can explore different interpretations, actions, and staging. Be very clear about your goals. If you are looking for producers or backers for a full production, you will need to focus on the final product. If you and the playwright are still working on the text, the workshop production may be used to continue the play development process. Either way, by moving to a production that is memorized and staged, the expectations for the workshop will be higher than for a reading.

Although actors usually do not get paid to rehearse and perform a reading or workshop, you should find it relatively easy to get actors to work on new material. In the professional theater world, acting in a reading or workshop is like an exclusive preaudition: It gives actors the opportunity to show what they can do with a role. Within a university or college, readings and workshops provide actors with performance opportunities that require minimal rehearsal time. There is a special excitement in being the first actor to play a role. With professional actors, however, you run the risk of losing actors to a paying acting job since you are not compensating them, so always have alternative actors in mind for such an emergency.

Dramaturgs

The position of dramaturg has a relatively short history in the United States as compared to Europe. Many of the dramaturg's functions have become more common with the establishment of regional resident professional theaters across the country. These days, trained dramaturgs work in a variety of capacities in professional and university theaters. Most professional theaters that produce new plays employ a **literary manager**, whose main responsibility is to read and evaluate new plays, develop artistic relationships with playwrights, and produce play readings and workshops. To a director, literary managers offer valuable connections for future work. In university theaters, you are more likely to collaborate with production dramaturgs.

Production dramaturgs serve a number of purposes, including artistic, research, and critical functions. As an artistic collaborator, a dramaturg may translate or adapt a script for a particular production, and may prepare what is known as a **dramaturg's protocol**, an extensive collection of background research, which might include any or all of the following:

- A biography of the playwright
- The history of the writing of the play
- A production history, describing how the play has been staged in the past
- A summary of important criticism written about the play
- Social, political, cultural, historical, and religious background essential to understanding the world of the play

If you are fortunate enough to have a dramaturg prepare a protocol for your production, he or she might suggest new interpretations of the play, help you better understand the play, or serve as a sounding board for production ideas. A good dramaturg can also be valuable as an in-house critic, attending rehearsals and answering questions about the play as they arise. These dramaturgical functions are especially valuable when directing a play set in a time, place, or environment that you don't know much about, or written in a style or form that you have not encountered before.

In America, dramaturgy has a short history. Not that many schools teach or train dramaturgs, and unfortunately, the practice of using dramaturgs in production is still not widespread, and a great many directors do not do detailed dramaturgical work themselves. If you are fortunate enough to have a trained dramaturg whom you trust, he or she can do a great deal of background research that you may not have time for, and if the dramaturg is talented and you work well together, he or she may suggest production ideas that help improve the discussion. In working with a dramaturg, the key for the director is to agree with the dramaturg on what he or she will be doing and how the two of you will work together. By and large, I don't recommend allowing the dramaturg to be a second director. Instead, encourage the dramaturg to meet with you regularly and attend rehearsals, so that he or she may have the chance to clarify things about the play and make suggestions about the production. Ultimately, the director must decide how to use this information.

Dramaturgs often help directors with many essential tasks, including:

- Evaluating various translations of a foreign play.
- Creating a detailed production history, so that the director can see how various choices might work.
- Researching background on the playwright, the playwright's other plays, criticism of the play, and social, political, cultural, historical, and religious background for the setting of the play or the time and place in which the playwright wrote the play.
- With a new play, a dramaturg is frequently involved in readings and revisions, similar to the work done in the first half of the twentieth century by "play doctors," experts brought in to help improve a play. These days this dramaturgical task is often overseen by a theater's literary manager, a job frequently held by a dramaturg.

Music Directors and Choreographers

Working on a musical or an opera presents a new set of challenges for the director. For one thing, there are more collaborators and more directing elements. For another, some of these elements are controlled or heavily influenced by the choices of other people: the composer, the musical director, and the choreographer. Whereas working with a living composer on a new work bears a great deal of similarity to working with a living playwright in terms of process, it's important to realize the control that a composer has over the rhythms and tempos of the production. After all, the composer has written the music to be performed in a particular tempo and with a particular rhythm. Therefore, directing musicals and operas is somewhat akin to having a co-director—the composer—make some of the choices about tempos, rhythms, moods, and even (implicit in the music) movement, and then working with and around those choices. It's a wonderful challenge that will force you to reconsider how you direct.

The music director and choreographer on these productions (unless the director takes on some of this work) can and should be your greatest assets. If you have good collaborators in these positions, you need not have an extensive background in music to direct a musical or opera. You need only to listen carefully to the score and to your collaborators, and be willing to accept more help in these areas. A good music director will make your directing look even better; a good choreographer can emphasize what you see as key moments—in musicals and operas these are often musical numbers, scenes, or arias—with breathtaking movement that serves the text, the score, and the action.

A Music Director Collaborates

As the director illuminates the core of the piece, the music director does the same for the score. In a musical it is the composer, and sometimes the lyricist, whom the audience remembers after the performance: Rodgers and Hammerstein, George and Ira Gershwin, Kander and Ebb, Sondheim. Few people can name the book writer of a musical play. The lyric is the common ground for the director, music director, and actor. The manner in which the composer joins words and music in time, space, and pitch gives clues to the characters' actions by creating a kind of "dictated line reading," which is anathema to many actors and directors when rehearsing the spoken word. Deciphering the dramatic clues in the sung and instrumental portions of the score is a musical detective's heaven, and a music director who is this type of musical and dramatic sleuth is priceless to the director. The director can use the music director's expertise to discover why the lyric is set as it is, how the pitches require the singing voice to operate effectively, and what the actor can do with the lyric as a result of the vocal requirements. The music director helps the director in dealing with how the tempo or the speed of the lyric's delivery affects what the character is doing in a situation that might have otherwise had a different interpretation if it did not have the indicated tempo or note values. A director should consider these points when conceiving a musical production as a whole. Ultimately, the director seeks a music director who can collaborate on a vision of the piece and help meld the music and action to achieve this vision.

Nathan Matthews is a professional music director, conductor, and composer, and the producing artistic director of the Riverside Opera Ensemble.

KEY TERMS

Staged reading.   A reading of a play in which the actors hold scripts in hand and move about the performance space as they might in a production. Their movements might be somewhat pared down compared to actual production, limited by the obstacle of holding the scripts and the shortened rehearsal period. Staged readings usually rehearse for less than one week.

Reading.   A seated reading of the play with no movement. The director's sole compositional task is to seat the actors in a formation that intensifies the characters' interactions; the formation may be minimally altered from scene to scene. Readings have little or no rehearsal time, therefore the director must quickly and concisely communicate his or her core action and central ideas about the script, which might include central conflicts, characterization, and key moments.

Workshop production.   A production in which the actors are off-book, with minimal technical and design support. The goal is usually to explore the potential of the play and showcase it for a future full production, within a limited budget and a rehearsal period of one to three weeks.

Literary manager. The staff member at a professional theater responsible for play development and dramaturgy, including finding and developing new scripts and translations through readings, staged readings, and workshops. The literary manager might oversee a staff that reads submitted plays and provides initial evaluations of the scripts' merits.

Production dramaturg. The dramaturg assigned to a production of a play, responsible for script development of a new play or translation, constructive in-house criticism through the rehearsal process, and/or writing program notes.

Dramaturg's protocol. A comprehensive research document containing background on the playwright, the play, its production history, dramatic criticism, and any other information relevant to understanding the play fully in its original context or within the production in process.

CHAPTER

7

Auditions and Casting

It may seem strange at first to think of an actor's audition as a collaboration. After all, the actor is trying out for job: a role in your production. Think of the audition as your first "test" collaboration. It is in your interest to create an environment in which every actor does his or her best work, so that you can choose the best actors for your ensemble. Yet the pressures of most audition situations are likely to hinder actors from doing their best work, and their desire to please directors might prevent them from collaborating to the best of their abilities during the audition. What can you do to help actors do their best work and show you the ways in which they might collaborate? The answer lies in a combination of the type of audition you hold and the way in which you conduct it.

The central goal of the audition is to determine which actors might be right for particular roles. If you have the luxury of auditioning different combinations of actors together (more common in university theater than in professional theater), you may also be able to see how the actors work together. You can also use auditions to find out other things about actors: how they take direction and adjust to your notes; how they answer questions about the character or the play; whether they react differently to various scene partners; what type of language they use to describe their artistic choices; and whether they treat everyone with respect. An actor's audition begins the minute the actor gets within earshot of the audition room; it does not end until he or she has left the premises. Watch each actor carefully before, during, and after each reading. Does the actor seem focused? Does he or she have a good attitude? What is the actor's reaction when he or she thinks a scene has not gone well?

I once auditioned two talented young actors for a scene showcase at a summer theater festival. The scene was between two brothers. The older brother berates the younger brother for disobeying his instructions to not leave the house. The two actors did a sizzling reading, a standout audition that instantly won me over. As they left the audition room, one actor turned to the other and began to curse at him violently. I was beginning to work with the next set of actors, but I stopped to listen to the commotion in the hallway. Could I cast an actor this voluble? Could these two actors work together and collaborate in an atmosphere of mutual respect?

I called in the actor who had been on the receiving end of this tirade first. When I asked him whether he believed he could work with the other actor, he nonchalantly replied, "Oh sure. He was just joking." I had to have a long talk with the first actor, the one who was "joking," about appropriate rehearsal behavior before I felt comfortable casting him in the scene. Ultimately, the scene succeeded, but we had to set the ground rules for collaboration before the first rehearsal. But once we set ground rules, I never had a problem with this actor again; in fact, he became one of my most dedicated collaborators. The lesson is a simple but crucial one: Pay attention to everything that happens in and around the audition space. Watch how your actors interact with one another; observe their body language; and listen to every word they say.

There are many ways you can find out more about your actors through the audition process, so let's go through the process step by step and examine the opportunities that arise along the way. Let's assume, for example, that for the initial audition you have asked the actors to prepare and present a brief monologue. Before an actor introduces himself or herself, you have the opportunity to speak with the person briefly as he or she enters the room. Although this is only a brief moment, it is a crucial one, because the actor is usually nervous. This is your chance to put actors at ease, learn their names, shake their hands, and answer any questions. It is also a brief window of opportunity for you to see the actors as people, not performers. Help the actors relax so that they will do their best work. Do not try to communicate significant information to actors before an audition. They are unlikely to remember anything you say at this particular moment. Save important information for the end of the audition; keep the beginning of the audition light and friendly; focus on establishing trust.

The actor will either hand you a headshot and resume or an audition sheet (see Appendix A for a sample audition sheet). There are several things to look for in these documents. What kind of roles has the actor played in the past? Has the actor played roles at your institution or theater before? Has the actor worked with directors or companies with whom you are familiar? Has he or she taken acting classes with anyone you know? Has the actor had significant training? Does the actor have any special skills that might be useful in this production? Is he or she able to do any dialects or accents? On the more practical side, does the actor have any significant conflicts with the rehearsal or performance schedule?

You might ask actors to stand toward the back of the acting space, so that you can get an idea of how well they project their voices. You can ask them to adjust the distance between the two of you to approximate the size of the theater in which you will be performing, within the confines of the audition space. You can even hold callbacks in a much larger space (or outdoors) to test the actors' vocal projection capabilities.

Some of the first things to write down during an audition include:

- Rough estimates of height, weight, and coloring, to help you remember the actor
- Unusual or noteworthy physical or vocal characteristics
- The pitch of the actor's voice: high, medium, or low
- Physical or vocal mannerisms that seem ingrained or habitual

If you see a repetitive mannerism, try to figure out whether it is part of the characterization or simply a nervous habit. Next, look at the substance of the audition piece. Is it clear to whom the actor is speaking? Do you get a sense of what the actor is trying to do to that person? Does he or she use the space well? Does the actor vary pitch, volume, tempo, and rhythm, so that the piece has an overall shape or rhythm that is consistent with its purpose?

At the end of the audition, always thank the actor. Auditions are difficult for everyone, so it's important to recognize every actor's effort. This way, actors are more likely to audition for you again, and any future collaborations with actors you don't cast this time around will start from a good place. Your reputation as a director and as a person to work with will be greatly influenced by the way you treat people during auditions, so be attentive, responsive, and kind, and don't let the power of your position or your single-minded pursuit of the best cast prevent you from interacting with the actors in a human and humane fashion.

EXERCISE

Mock audition. Using class members as "auditioners," take turns running a mock audition. Each of you should take a turn or two bringing an actor into the audition, introducing yourself, briefly explaining what the actor should expect, introducing the other directors, and then thanking the actor at the end of the audition. The audition itself can simply consist of the "actor" saying a single sentence. After each audition, the class should give the director feedback on what worked best, what put the actor at ease, and what things the director should work on.

Casting the One-Act Plays

When the class conducts auditions for real, all of the directors should take turns conducting the first audition, which may consist of a monologue, cold reading, or improvisation. The directors should then each hold callbacks, followed by a class casting session, in which the directors negotiate the casts for their plays. If you have enough people audition, try to avoid casting actors in more than one play, as it is demoralizing for your acting pool.

Callbacks provide the opportunity for you to work with actors in more depth and get a sense of how they might collaborate with you and others in rehearsal. Whereas the initial audition may give you some sense of whether an actor is appropriate for a particular role, the callback allows you to see how actors work together and discover how different combinations of actors might work together. It is in your best interests to see as many possible combinations of actors as possible. First, you never know for sure what the best combination might be until you try it. Second, seeing each actor with a variety of partners will tell you quite a bit about how the actors adapt to different partners. If an actor is truly listening and reacting to his or her partners, the performance should change from partner to partner. Last, a director never knows when an actor may be unavailable for the role, due to another obligation or production. Therefore, always keep more than one actor in mind for each role. I recommend calling back three to four actors for each role.

One way to look at a wide range of combinations of actors is to use what I call a **tag audition**. Bring in all the actors you are considering for a pair of roles. Start with two actors, but give copies of the scene (**sides**) to all the actors. After watching the first pairing for a minute or less, "tag" one of the other actors. They should then slide into the appropriate role in the scene and pick up the scene at that point. In the course of five minutes, you can get a brief look at all the possible combinations of actors in these two roles. As you're watching, mark down the best combinations, and then bring those pairs back for a complete reading of the scene.

Audition Goals

- Be sure to create a relaxed and safe environment that encourages your actors to do their best work.
- Keep an eye out for indications of the actors' attitudes toward the work. Look for good collaborators who are willing to take risks and are not discouraged when a choice doesn't work.
- Test the actor's ability to collaborate with you and other actors.
- Evaluate what role the actor best fits within your interpretation.
- Note all significant vocal, physical, and psychological characteristics.
- When looking at monologues, focus on the clarity of each actor's interpretation. The monologue serves as an example of the actor's finished work.
- Improvisation exercises are usually used in auditions as a way of judging each actor's ability to be spontaneous. Use improvisation if it seems appropriate to the play or your approach to the play.
- In watching cold readings (particularly during callbacks), encourage actors to look up from the page and interact with their scene partners. Focus on observing the actors' relationships.

■ Always thank the auditioners for their time and effort. Actors put themselves on the line every time they audition, and they deserve your appreciation. Moreover, by showing your respect and thanks for their work, they are more likely to audition for you again and encourage others to audition. You never know when a particular actor will be right for a production. Build your pool of future talent by treating all auditioners with respect.

SUPPLEMENTAL READING

Ball, William, *A Sense of Direction*. New York: Drama Books, 1984.
Merlin, Joanna. *Auditioning: An Actor-Friendly Guide*. New York: Vintage, 2001.
Shurtleff, Michael. *Audition*. New York: Walker, 1980.

APPENDIX A

Forms

Project Proposal Form

Director _____

Play and playwright _____

Faculty advisor _____ Cast: _____ male and _____ female roles

Proposed performance space _____

Proposed rehearsal schedule _____

Proposed performance dates _____

Minimal technical requirements _____

Budget needs (including cost of rights, scripts, photocopies, technical elements, etc.):

_____

_____

_____

What do you see as the core action of the play? How do you intend to achieve this with minimal technical support? You may continue your explanation on an attached page.

_____

_____

_____

_____

_____

_____

_____

_____

_____

_____

_____

_____

_____

Previous directing experience (list play/playwright/venue and courses taken):

_____

_____

_____

Sample Audition Notice

[Title of play]
by [playwright]

Directed by [director]

To be performed:
[Theater]
[Performance dates]

Rehearsals begin: [date]

Auditions will be held in the Center for the Arts rehearsal room on Friday, [date] from 5–8:30 pm. If you would like to read the script beforehand, copies are available on reserve in the Undergraduate Library. Please prepare a two-minute monologue, preferably [choose one: modern, classical, comedic, in verse]. You many sign up in advance for an audition time below.

5:00	6:45
5:05	6:50
5:10	BREAK
5:15	7:00
5:20	7:05
5:25	7:10
5:30	7:15
5:35	7:20
5:40	7:25
5:45	7:30
5:50	7:35
BREAK	7:40
6:00	7:45
6:05	BREAK
6:10	8:00
6:15	8:05
6:20	8:10
6:25	8:15
6:30	8:20
6:35	8:25
6:40	8:30

If you are unable to audition at these times, please contact [director or stage manager, telephone number, e-mail] to arrange an alternative audition time. Callbacks will be held on Saturday from 1–5 pm. Please check the callboard for callback information and audition sides at 10 pm following the night of the first audition.

Audition Form

NAME_____ HEIGHT_____

E-MAIL_____ HAIR_____

PHONE_____ (home) _____ (cell) EYES_____

MAJOR_____ YEAR_____

Acting Experience

Role_____ Play_____ Theater/Director_____

Acting Classes

Class_____ Instructor_____ Semester_____

Special skills (dialects, dance, music, etc.):

Days and times you are unavailable for rehearsal:

Physical limitations or injuries:

Please write down your schedule for classes and activities on the back of this page.

Sample Callback Form

My thanks to all who auditioned for this show. It was a pleasure to see your work, and I appreciate the time and effort everyone took in preparing their audition pieces. I'd like to see the following people for callbacks. Listed below are the people I've called back, the sides I'd like you to cold-read Sunday, and the times you are called. Please pick up the sides below and review and prepare them in advance.

Some of you may be called for more than one role or asked to read with more than one scene partner. I encourage you to do your best work in every reading to maximize the chance of being cast. If you come to the callback, I will assume that you will accept the role if cast. Please call the stage manager as soon as possible if you are unavailable for casting.

1 pm, side A:	John:	David Fredricksen, Eric Kennedy, Mike Rosen
	Abby:	Jenna Braun, Ashley Bueller, Valerie Smith
2 pm, side B:	John:	David Fredricksen, Eric Kennedy, Mike Rosen
	Lizzy:	Angela Knapp, Zoe Peterson, Danielle Seitzman
3 pm, side C:	Sgt. Heard:	Richard Leon, Michael Roberts
	Dr. Wisker:	Jeff Leary, Dan Post
4 pm, side D:	Mr. Puffer:	Franklin Davis, Dan Post
	Agnes:	Jane Calvert, Karen Linder
5 pm, side E:	Narrator:	Jenna Braun, Ashley Bueller, Valerie Smith

I expect to post the cast list by Monday morning at noon, assuming there are no conflicts. Please check the callboard at that time for the cast list or updated information. If you were not called back, please check the cast list on Monday anyhow; some of you may be cast in smaller roles without a callback.

I look forward to seeing more of your work tomorrow, and I encourage all of you to continue auditioning for and attending our productions. If you'd like to be involved with this production in any other capacity, please contact me or my stage manager.

Many thanks,
The Director

Sample Cast List

Thank you to all who auditioned. The strong work I saw in auditions and call-backs made the job of casting this show more difficult, but ultimately better. To all of you who did not get cast, I encourage you to continue auditioning. The following is the cast list. Please initial next to your name to indicate acceptance of the role. The first read-through will be held this Wednesday at 7 pm in the Green Room. Please pick up your copy of the script before then at the departmental office.

JOHN	Mike Rosen
ABBY	Ashley Bueller
LIZZY	Angela Knapp
SGT. HEARD	Michael Roberts
DR. WISKER	Dan Post
MR. PUFFER	Franklin Davis
AGNES	Jane Calvert
NARRATOR	Jenna Braun
ENSEMBLE	Valerie Smith
	Jeff Leary
	Wendy Hanson
	Justin Hockney

Thanks again to all who auditioned for your hard work,
The Director

Rehearsal Observation Form

Play_____

Director_____

Place and period of observation_____

Rehearsal #____ of ____. On or off-book?____ Blocked?____ Unit or run?_____

What seems to be the primary goal of the rehearsal? Was it met? What other approaches might the director consider?

Describe one interaction in which the director collaborated well and one in which he or she had difficulty collaborating or missed an opportunity to do so.

Describe how the director most effectively encouraged the ensemble to contribute ideas to the process and one occasion in which he or she had difficulty doing so.

Describe the director's personal use of space: how he or she sat and moved in the space during the rehearsal, his or her physical relationship to the actors at various times, and the reaction of the actors to the director's use of space.

Producing Checklist

When you first began directing, you will probably find yourself producing your work as well. I have included a brief checklist below of tasks that you may have to take on to successfully produce your play.

❏ Secure the performance rights
❏ Secure performance space
❏ Reserve audition and rehearsal space
❏ Hire designers, a stage manager, and technical staff
❏ Determine technical/design needs
❏ Draw up a production budget
❏ Assemble publicity materials, such as a press release
❏ Design, print, and distribute posters (see Appendix A for necessary information)
❏ Design and print programs (see Appendix A for required information)

Program Information

There are many ways to design and lay out a program. One of the least expensive and yet most impressive formats is to use a simple 8½-by-11-inch page folded in half and printed on both sides like a greeting card. This format provides you with four pages: a cover page, two interior pages, and a back page. The program is an important document because its quality creates an expectation for the production. It also serves to document your work and acknowledge all your collaborators. You should include most or all of the following information, though you will probably rearrange the information to present it in a visually pleasing and efficient order:

Cover: Title, image (usually taken from the poster for consistency), performance dates, producing company, venue, and any major sponsoring organizations or companies

Page 2 (left inside page): Title, playwright, director, cast, designers, intermission, place, time, setting

Page 3 (right inside page): Staff, including the stage managers, crew, technical staff, house manager, and others; director's or dramaturg's notes

Page 4 (back page): Special thanks, other acknowledgments, upcoming events; permanent staff, faculty, or supervisors

Poster Information

Depending upon your budget, the posters for your production might be anything from 8½-by-11-inch black-and-white photocopies to larger, full-color photocopies or prints. Color photocopying and digital photography and printing have become quite inexpensive, putting quality posters within the reach of most people. Focus, though, on the impact of the poster, the "bang for the buck" rather than the most expensive product. What, then, makes a poster eye-catching and what information should be included on any poster?

A good poster should attract attention, while giving potential audience members some idea of what the production is about. You need to find a central image, either by drawing one (if you are artistically inclined or have a friend who is) or by photographing one (digital photography allows you more freedom to manipulate the image or create photomontages). It may also help you to include some of the names of your cast in the poster. Particularly on college campuses, much of your audience will attend because they know a cast member.

All posters should include the following information:

- Play title, playwright, director, designers, and producing organization
- A central image
- Date, time, and place of performances
- Cost of tickets
- Reservation policy and telephone number for information or reservations

You might also consider including a quote from the play or intriguing catchphrase for the production.

Course Outline

Week	Topic	Reading and exercises due
1	**What is directing?** Action, collaboration, play selection	Read Introduction; Assign scene directing partners
2	**Script analysis:** Language, character analysis	Read *Betrayal*, Ch. 1: Collaboration and Leadership; Ch. 4 "Language" and "Character"
3	**Script analysis:** Dramatic action, units of action	Read Ch. 2: Core Action; Ch. 4 "Structure" and "Shifts and Key Moments"; *Character analysis* due
4	**Working with actors:** Actions and objectives	Read Ch. 3: Rehearsal Collaboration; Ch. 4; "Actions/Objectives" and "Relationship and Status"; *Final project proposals* due; *Unit breakdown* due
5	**Groundplans**	Read Ch. 4: "Groundplan"; *Actions/objectives and core action* due
6	**Open rehearsals:** Midterm scenes	*Groundplan* due; *Approval of final project* due
7	**Midterm scene presentations**	*Scene script analysis* due
8	**Auditions and casting**	Read Ch. 7: "Auditions and Casting"; *Core action statement* due; *Final play analysis and groundplan* due one week before rehearsal starts
9	**Early rehearsals for final plays:** Preparation, focus, survival	*Hold Auditions; A program rehearsal starts*
10	**Movement and gesture**	Read Ch. 4: "Movement" and "Gesture"; *B program rehearsal starts*
11	**Tempo/Rhythm/Environment**	Read Ch. 4: "Tempo and Rhythm" and "Environment"; *C program rehearsal starts*
12	**Visual composition**	Read Ch. 4: "Visual Composition"; *A program performances*
13	**Sound, mood, and style**	Read Ch. 4: "Sound and Mood" and "Style"; *B program performances*
14	**Tech and dress rehearsals:** Preparation and goals	Read Ch. 6: "Design Timetable"; *C performances*

Final critiques during final exam period

Performance schedule:
- A program (week 12): 3–5 short plays
- B program (week 13): 3–5 short plays
- C program (week 14): 3–5 short plays

APPENDIX B

Glossary of Key Terms

Action. What one character is doing to another character. It should be a playable verb: a concrete action that an actor can pursue for several minutes. It should also be an active and easy to understand verb, something we would use in everyday conversation.

Asymmetrical compositions. The characters' positions do not form a symmetrical pattern but may still find balance through angles, variety, and relative weight. Asymmetrical compositions tend to be more dynamic and less formal; if unbalanced, an asymmetrical composition may suggest disorder or chaos.

Balanced compositions. Stage compositions that find equilibrium through the placement of the relative weights of different objects and people on stage. Not every composition needs to be balanced, but directors should always be aware of the effect of the balance or imbalance of a composition on the shape of the action. Asymmetrical compositions (see above) can still find balance through a combination of the weight and number of forms on stage. For example, a single large form upstage left might be balanced by several small forms downstage right—asymmetrical, but balanced.

Blocking. Historically, blocking refers to the planned movement of actors on stage from one "block" of the stage to another. In recent theater practice, blocking can be preplanned by the director, created by the ensemble, or the result of a collaboration between the actors and the director.

Business. Small movements by the actors, usually involving the use of stage properties. Business provides physical action for the actors, which can be used to reveal a character's inner state, through the choice of business and the way in which the character performs the business, as when a nervous character repeatedly straightens up a room.

Callbacks. A second audition for a production, during which the director can work with actors in greater depth, discuss the role with them, and look at different combinations of actors.

Composition. The arrangement of actors on stage within the **frame.**

Core action. The director's choice of the central elements, within or inspired by the text, that will fuel a particular production of a play for the ensemble. The core action should be based on an understanding of the text, but it can emphasize whatever elements the director finds central to his or her interpretation. It will vary from director to director, depending upon the director's ideas, the production space, the cast, and the community for which the play is being produced.

Costume parade. Usually held early in the technical rehearsal process, the costume parade provides the director with the opportunity to sit down with the costume designer and see the costumes under the actual lighting, uninterrupted by other concerns.

Countering. The convention of actors balancing their stage positions in reaction to the entrance or movement of another actor or group of actors on stage. Countering contributes greatly to the ability to move from composition to composition smoothly.

153

Cue-to-cue.   Before the advent of computerized light boards, the first technical rehearsal was normally a "cue-to-cue"—a rehearsal in which the ensemble jumped from one cue to the next, skipping the material in between. Some lighting designers still employ this method, although most prefer to create the cues during a run-through. Computerized light boards have made this much easier to do, and creating the cues as the actors perform allows the designers and technical staff to time the cues so that they blend with the action on stage.

Directing elements.   Refers to fundamental building blocks that help directors achieve their interpretations. Directing elements shape the pattern of a play in production in the same way that a piece of music is shaped by the tones, notes, rhythms, melodies, harmonies, and conductor's choices, or a painting is shaped by the painter's use of size, shape, color, patterns, and the relationships among these.

Dramaturg.   A dramaturg functions as the director's extra set of critical eyes: someone who has done extensive research on the play, the playwright, the writing and world of the play, and its genre, for example, so that he or she can critique the work in progress. Dramaturgs may function as critical and research support for a production, adapt or translate a text, or run the literary management department of a resident theater (coordinating readings, workshops, and playwrights' retreats).

Dramaturg's protocol.   A comprehensive research document containing background on the playwright, the play, its production history, dramatic criticism, and any other information relevant to understanding the play fully in its original context or within the production in process.

Dress rehearsals.   The last two or three rehearsals will be dress rehearsals; the very last rehearsal before opening might be used as an open or invited dress rehearsal, so that the cast starts to become used to the presence of an audience and how that may affect their performances. At this point, all costumes are added to the production, and last-minute touches on the set and adjustments to the lighting should become finalized.

Dynamic composition.   The visual interest created by the use of angles, levels, and positional tension in a composition. Dynamic compositions tend to make greater use of angles, or irregular triangles created by several characters or groups, and of actors standing on different levels or creating levels by virtue of some characters sitting and others standing.

Ensemble-created sound.   Sound that the actors or crew make themselves, through the use of their voices, bodies, instruments, or percussion.

Environmental sound.   Any sound that can be justified by the environment that the playwright specifies or the director chooses as a setting, such as the sound of traffic and people in a street scene, or the ocean in a beach scene. Compare to **underscoring.**

Found space.   The use of an existing, non-theatrical space for a production. Many avant-garde productions have experimented with the use of spaces other than theaters. Such spaces can be used naturalistically or as a stylized counterpoint to the action.

Frame.   Any device by which a portion of the stage area is delineated as the playing space. The most apparent frame is a proscenium arch, which serves as a literal picture frame around the action. Frames can be created and may even shift during the course of a production by using lighting, legs, drops, scenery, or even human bodies to limit the playing space to a selected area of the stage. The frame of a composition is always a factor, whether observed formally, broken purposefully, or alternated for effect.

Gesture. The characters' body language, particularly their hand movements. Gesture functions on at least two levels: *societal gestures* tell the audience something about the perceived norms of the society; *individual gestures* reveal how particular characters fit into the society, their self-concept, and their feelings at any particular moment. *Personal gestures* are unique to the individual; *psychological gestures* reveal something deeper about character.

Groundplan. A top view of the stage space, drawn to scale, within which the production's action will occur, indicating the exact placement of all walls, stairs, levels, windows, doors, and large properties such as furniture.

Key moment. The most important moment of the play or scene, usually the last moment of major conflict. In the progression of key moments that marks the shape of a play, the major key moment is the climax—the moment at which the conflict reaches its final clash, the highest point in the arc of the action.

Lighting looks. Sketches drawn by the lighting designer to communicate to the director and the other designers how the lighting should look in each scene or key moment.

Light plot. The lighting designer's blueprint indicating the position, direction, color, and type of each lighting instrument to be used in the production is called the light plot. From the light plot, the lighting designer should be able to tell the director and the design team how various parts of the stage will be lit during each scene.

Literary manager. Staff member at a professional theater responsible for play development and dramaturgy, including finding and developing new scripts and translations through readings, staged readings, and workshops. The literary manager might oversee a staff that reads submitted plays and provides an initial evaluation of the scripts' merits.

Objective. Something a character wants, needs, or desires from another character.

Off-book. When the actors run a scene, act, or the play without script in hand, having memorized all their lines, they are "off-book." In reality, the first rehearsal off-book often seems to be a step back for the production, since much of the work of the early rehearsals will temporarily disappear as actors focus on their lines. This is a part of the process, and the director, while firmly requiring the actors to learn their lines in a timely fashion, must be patient until the early work reemerges following successful memorization.

Pacing. The overall flow of the action in a play, which should give the sense that the tempos and rhythms of individual units or scenes fit together in some way, moving the action from scene to scene effortlessly. Pacing can help bridge the gaps between scenes.

Paper tech. A sit-down meeting approximately a week before the production moves into the theater, during which the director, stage manager, lighting designer, and sound designer pencil in rough cues for the production.

Photo call. Most companies or producers photograph productions for archival and publicity purposes. These photographs are often take in a special photo call rather than during a run-through, so that the photographer may change angles, lenses, or even ask for the intensity of the lighting to be increased to improve the photo. A director can use these photos to create a portfolio of his or her work for future employers.

Picturization.   The use of visual composition to convey a situation, relationship, or story. Picturization can convey story and relationship, whether the director preplans the composition or finds it with the ensemble in rehearsal.

Plot.   The playwright's selection and ordering of events from the story that occur on stage. Plot need not be chronological; by its nature, it includes only a portion of the complete chronological story.

Poor theater.   Originally coined by the Polish experimental director Jerzy Grotowski, poor theater, in a more general sense, refers to productions that depend upon the virtuosity of the actors and utilize a minimal amount of technical and design support to achieve their goals.

Reading.   A seated reading of the play with no movement. The director's sole compositional task is to seat the actors in a formation that intensifies the characters' interactions; the formation may be minimally altered from scene to scene. Readings have little or no rehearsal time; therefore the director must quickly and concisely communicate his or her core action and central ideas about the script, which might include objectives, key conflicts, characterization, and key moments.

Relationship.   A relationship between two characters can be described in terms of generic type—best friends, mother–daughter, boss–worker—and in terms of the specifics of the relationship at that moment. Not every mother–daughter relationship is the same, and even a single relationship varies depending upon the circumstances of the moment.

Rhythm.   The pattern of the beat of a unit, scene, or play. It can be used to describe the pulse of a unit or the overall pattern created from scene to scene throughout a play. Rhythm therefore can be described on many levels: from the smallest (the rhythm of a page or less of dialogue) to the largest (the overall rhythm of the play).

Scale.   When a model is built to scale, this means that a unit of measurement of the model represents a larger unit on the actual set. One-quarter-inch scale means that every ½ inch on the model equals 1 foot on the set; ½-inch scale means that every ½ inch on the model equals 1 foot on the set. By measuring the model, the director can figure out exactly how large something will be on a real set.

Scale model.   A model of the set built to ¼- or ½-inch scale, so that each ¼ or ½ inch on the model equals 1 foot of the actual stage space.

Shape.   The pattern or arc created by the ensemble's development of all the elements of production, from acting and music to rhythm and tempo to colors and textures. A compelling shape should communicate your vision most effectively.

Shifts.   Shifts occur anytime a character changes his or her action in a significant way. Although a script may imply shifts at particular moments in the play, the choice of action and its placement in a scene is ultimately a matter of script analysis and interpretation that is decided upon by the actor and the director.

Sides.   A copy of a section of a scene for use in auditions. A director usually selects short sides, ranging from one to three pages, that challenge actors to meet the various demands of the roles and give the director a chance to see actors in scenes with important character combinations.

Sound plot.   A written set of sound cues for a production, with specific notations as to when each sound cue will be called during each scene.

Spine.   Term coined by Harold Clurman to refer to the throughline of a production. Spine is the equivalent to "core action," though it connotes a greater sense of linear narrative and therefore works better for traditional narrative than for experimental or episodic plays.

Staged reading.   A reading of a new play with basic blocking but "script-in-hand" (lines not memorized), intended either to demonstrate the stage-worthiness of a play to a theater or producer or to help the playwright revise the script.

Status.   A character's feeling of superiority or inferiority in relationship to another character. Status is affected by social and economic factors, such as wealth and employment, but these do not definitively determine a character's status. A servant may be high status in relationship to a weaker master, for example. What happens between characters affects status as well, so that status in always shifting.

Story.   All the information a play provides about the events that occur on and off stage. Story is chronological and includes all events before, during, and after the action of a play.

Style.   Everything that brings the world of the play together, including the use of language, manners, environment, gestures, movement, sounds, relationships, and even the overall rhythm of the world of the play.

Stylized sound.   When the script calls for sound or the director adds sound that does not occur naturally in the setting. This can be **underscoring** or can involve more aggressive uses of sound.

Super-objective.   The single driving need, want, or desire of each character over the course of the entire play.

Symmetrical compositions.   Such compositions exhibit a visual pattern and tend to imply formality or rigidity, as in a courtroom or a military formation.

Tag audition.   A cold reading of a scene in which various actors under consideration for the two or more parts being read can be shuttled in and out of the scene by the director. On a sign from the director, an actor tags the actor playing a role and takes his or her place in the scene. This audition format allows the director to see a great variety of combinations of actors in a brief time.

Technical rehearsals.   Near the end of the rehearsals period, two or three rehearsals are devoted to technical rehearsals. During this time, the technical elements of the production will gradually be introduced, first the lighting cues and the set, followed by (or in concert with) the sound cues.

Tempo.   The speed of a scene or unit. It may be described in any language that captures the sense of the speed, including music terminology, beats per minute, or by playing music or a metronome.

Thumbnail sketches.   In the early stages of the design process, designers may draw rough sketches in miniature, slightly bigger than a postage stamp, to communicate their initial design ideas to the director and to one another

Transitions.   Within any director's unit breakdown of a play transitions will be needed to bridge the gap between one unit of action and another. It's important for a director to find the transitions between units so that the overall action of a production appears to be seemless.

Underscoring.   The use of music underneath the spoken dialogue; in other words, music that can be heard without obscuring the actors' dialogue. Whereas environmental sound provides the ambience for a scene, underscoring is often more directly related to the action, not only serving to create an atmosphere, but also supporting the action and overall shape of a scene or unit.

Unit breakdown.   The practice of breaking down a play into smaller units, which can be used in rehearsal and reflect the director's understanding of the structure of the play.

Visual composition.   The placement of actors on the stage in relationship to one another, to the set, and to the audience. The changes in visual composition from moment to moment create a series of visual pictures that help establish the rhythm or shape of the production.

White model.   A scale model of the set in white, in order to show the use of space before all the designers agree upon a color palate for the production.

Workshop production.   A production in which the actors are off-book, with minimal technical and design support. The goal is usually to explore the potential of the play and showcase it for a future full production, within a limited budget and a rehearsal period of one to three weeks.

APPENDIX C

Bibliography of One-Act Plays

Alexander, Robert, et al. *Heaven and Hell (on Earth), a Divine Comedy: Short Plays from Actors Theatre of Louisville: A Comic Anthology*. New York: Dramatists Play Service, 2002.

Allen, Woody. *Three One-Act Plays: Riverside Drive, Old Saybrook, Central Park West*. New York: Random House, 2003.

Ball, Allan. *Five One Act Plays*. New York: Dramatists Play Service, 1998.

Bert, Deb and Norman, eds. *New One-Plays for Acting Students: Anthology of Short One-Act Plays for One, Two, or Three Actors*. Colorado Springs: Meriwether, 2003.

———. *One-Act Plays for Acting Students*. Colorado Springs: Meriwether, 1990.

———. *Play It Again! More One-Act Plays for Acting Students*. Colorado Springs: Meriwether, 1993.

Brown, Kent R., ed. *25 in 10 : Twenty-five Ten-Minute Plays*. Woodstock, IL: Dramatic Publishing, 2002.

Carden, William, ed. *HB Playwrights Short Play Festival: The Airport Plays 1999*. Hanover, NH: Smith and Kraus, 2002.

———. *HB Playwrights Short Play Festival: The Funeral Plays 2000*. Hanover, NH: Smith and Kraus, 2002.

———. *HB Playwrights Short Play Festival: The Motel Plays 1997*. Hanover, NH: Smith and Kraus, 2002.

———. *HB Playwrights Short Play Festival: The Museum Plays 1998*. Hanover, NH: Smith and Kraus, 2002.

Cerf, Bennett, and Van H. Cartmell, eds. *24 Favorite One-Act Plays*. New York: Main Street Books, reissued 1963.

Chandler, Wilma Marcus, and John Howie Patterson, eds. *Eight Tens @ Eight Festivals: Thirty 10-minute Plays from the Santa Cruz Festivals I-VI*. Hanover, NH: Smith and Kraus, 2001.

Chekhov, Anoton. *Five Comic One-Act Plays*. Dover, 1999.

Delgado, Ramôan, ed. *The Best Short Plays, 1983*. Radnor, PA: Chilton Book, 1983.

Dixon, Michael Bigelow, ed. *2002: The Best Ten-Minute Plays for 3 or More Actors*. Hanover, NH: Smith and Kraus, 2004.

Dixon, Michael Bigelow, and Liz Engelman, eds. *Ten-Minute Plays: Volume 4 from Actors Theatre of Louisville* (includes an article about teaching the ten-minute play). New York: Samuel French, 1998.

Dixon, Michael Bigelow, Tanya Palmer, and Brendan Healy, eds. *30 Ten-Minute Plays for 4, 5, and 6 Actors from Actors Theatre of Louisville's National Ten-Minute Play Contest*. Hanover, NH: Smith and Kraus, 2001.

Dixon, Michael Bigelow, and Michele Volansky, eds. *Ten-Minute Plays: Volume 3 from Actors Theatre of Louisville*. New York: Samuel French, 1995.

Dixon, Michael Bigelow, Amy Wegener, and Stephen Moulds, eds. *30 Ten-Minute Plays for 3 Actors from Actors Theatre of Louisville's National Ten-Minute Play Contest.* Hanover, NH: Smith and Kraus, 2001.

Dixon, Michael Bigelow, Amy Wegener, and Karen C. Petruska, eds. *30 Ten-Minute Plays for 2 Actors from Actors Theater of Louisville's National Ten-Minute Play Contest.* Hanover, NH: Smith and Kraus, 2001.

Durang, Christopher, ed. *27 Short Plays.* Hanover, NH: Smith and Kraus, 1996.

Ehn, Erik. *Erotic Curtsies.* Los Angeles: Green Integer, 2003.

———. *The Saint Plays.* Baltimore: Johns Hopkins University Press, 2000.

Ensemble Studio Theatre Marathon 2000: The Complete One-Act Plays. New York: Faber and Faber, 2001.

Ensemble Studio Theatre Marathon '99: The One-Act Plays. New York: Faber and Faber, 2000.

Ensemble Studio Theatre Marathon '84: The One-Act Plays. New York: Faber and Faber, 1985.

France, Rachel, ed. *A Century of Plays by American Women.* New York: Richards Rosen, 1979.

Germann, Greg, Cassandra Medley, and Laura Cahill, eds. *Three by E.S.T.: Three One-Act Plays Presented by Ensemble Studio Theatre.* New York: Dramatists Play Service, 1997.

Halpern, Daniel, ed. *Plays in One Act.* 2nd ed. Hopewell, NJ: Ecco, 1999.

Hurston, Zora Neale, Eulalie Spence, and Marita Bonner, et al. *The Prize Plays and Other One-Acts Published in Periodicals.* New York: G.K. Hall; London: Prentice Hall International, 1996.

Ives, David. *All in the Timing: Fourteen Plays.* New York: Vintage, 1994.

———. *Mere Mortals: Six One-Act Comedies.* New York: Dramatists Play Service, 1998.

———. *Lives of the Saints: Seven One-Act Plays.* New York: Dramatists Play Service, 2000.

———. *Take Ten II: More Ten-Minute Plays.* New York: Vintage, 2003.

———. *Time Flies and Other Short Plays.* New York: Grove, 2001.

Ives, David, and Nina Shengold, eds. *Take Ten: New Ten-Minute Plays.* New York: Vintage, 1997.

Lane, Eric, ed. *Telling Tales: New One-Act Plays.* New York: Penguin, 1993.

May, Elaine, and Alan Arkin. *Power Plays.* New York: Samuel French, 1999.

Melfi, Leonard. *Encounters: Six One-Act Plays.* New York: Samuel French, 1967.

Pape, Ralph. *Girls We Have Known and Other One-Act Plays.* New York: Samuel French, 1998.

Pinero, Miguel. *Outrageous One Act Plays.* Houston: Arte Publico, 1986.

Reed, John, Neith Boyce, and George Cram Cook, et al. *The Provincetown Plays: Second Series.* Reprint of the 1916 ed. published by I. Shay, New York. Great Neck, NY: Core Collection, 1976.

Richards, Stanley, ed. *Best Short Plays of the World Theatre, 1958–1967.* New York: Crown, 1968.

Roth, Ari, Leslie Ayvazian, and Keith Alan Benjamin. *Three More by E.S.T. '98.* New York: Dramatists Play Service, 1999.

Shanley, John Patrick. *13 by Shanley.* New York: Applause, 2000.

———. *Welcome to the Moon and Other Plays.* New York: Dramatists Play Service, 1998.

Slaight, Craig, ed. *New Plays from A.C.T.'s Young Conservatory, Vols. 1–4.* Lyme, NH: Smith and Kraus, 1993–2003.

Smith, Marisa, ed. *Act One '95: The Complete Plays*. Lyme, NH: Smith and Kraus, 1996.

———. *EST Marathon 1998: The One-Act Plays*. Lyme, NH: Smith and Kraus, 1999.

———. *EST Marathon 1997: The One-Act Plays*. Lyme, NH: Smith and Kraus, 1998.

———. *EST Marathon 1996: The One-Act Plays*. Lyme, NH: Smith and Kraus, 1995.

———. *EST Marathon 1995: The Complete One-Act Plays*. Lyme, NH: Smith and Kraus, 1995.

———. *EST Marathon 1994: One-Act Plays*. Lyme, NH: Smith and Kraus, 1995.

———. *Showtime's Act One Festival of One-Act Plays, 1994*. Lyme, NH: Smith and Kraus, 1995.

Twenty-Five Ten-Minute Plays from Actors Theater of Louisville. New York: Samuel French, 1989.

Volansky, Michele, and Michael Bigelow Dixon, eds. *20/20: Twenty One-Act Plays from Twenty Years of the Humana Festival*. Lyme, NH: Smith and Kraus, 1995.

Wasserstein, Wendy. *Seven One-Act Plays*. New York: Dramatists Play Service, 1999.

Wood, Gerald C., ed. *Selected One-Act Plays of Horton Foote*. Dallas: Southern Methodist University Press, 1989.

Wright, Doug, ed. *Unwrap Your Candy: An Evening of One-Act Plays*. New York: Dramatists Play Service, 2002.

Yeaton, Dana, ed. *Blasts from the Future: An Anthology of Ten-Minute Plays from the Vermont Young Playwrights Project*. Rochester, VT: Penstroke Press, 1999.

Young, Glenn, ed. *The Best American Short Plays, 1999–2000*. New York: Applause, 2001.

———. *The Best American Short Plays, 1998–1999*. New York: Applause, 2001.

———. *The Best American Short Plays, 1996–1997*. New York: Applause, 1998.

APPENDIX D

Selected Bibliography

Directing

Albright, Hardi. *Stage Direction in Transition*. Encino, CA: Dickenson, 1972.

Allen, Ralph, and John Gassner. *Theatre and Drama in the Making*. New York: Applause, 1992.

Ball, William. "Give the Audience a Chance." *Theatre Arts* 45 (1961).

———. *A Sense of Direction*. New York: Drama Books, 1984.

Barrault, Jean-Louis. *Reflections on the Theatre*. Barbara Well, trans. London: Rockliff, 1951.

———. *The Theatre of Jean-Louis Barrault*. New York: Hill and Wang, 1962.

Bartow, Arthur. *The Director's Voice: Twenty-One Interviews*. New York: Theatre Communications Group, 1988.

Benedetti, Robert. *The Director at Work*. Boston: Allyn and Bacon, 1985.

Black, George. *Contemporary Stage Direction*. New York: Holt, Rinehart and Winston, 1991.

Black, Malcolm. *First Reading to First Night: A Candid Look at Stage Directing*. Seattle: University of Washington Press, 1976.

Boetz, N. M. *The Director as Artist: Play Direction Today*. New York: Holt, Rinehart and Winston, 1987.

Bradby, David, and David Williams. *Directors' Theatre*. New York: St. Martin's, 1988.

Catron, Louis. *The Director's Vision: Play Direction from Analysis to Production*. Mountain View, NJ: Mayfield, 1989.

Clurman, Harold. *On Directing*. New York: Macmillan, 1972.

———. "Principles of Interpretation." In John Gassner, *Producing the Play*. New York: Dryden, 1953.

Coe, Robert. "The Extravagant Mysteries of Robert Wilson." *American Theatre* 2 (October 1985).

———. "What Makes Sellars Run." *American Theatre* 4 (December 1987).

Cohen, Robert, and John Harrop. *Creative Play Direction*. Englewood Cliffs, NJ: Prentice-Hall, 1984.

Cole, Susan Letzler. *Directors in Rehearsal: A Hidden World*. New York: Routledge, Chapman and Hall, 1992.

Cole, Toby, and Helen K. Chinoy. *Directors on Directing*. Rev. ed. Indianapolis: Bobbs Merrill, 1963.

Daniels, Rebecca. *Women Stage Directors Speak: Exploring the Influence of Gender on Their Work*. Jefferson, NC: McFarland, 1996.

Dean, Alexander, and Lawrence Carra. *Fundamentals of Play Directing*. New York: Holt, Rinehart and Winston, 1989.

Dietrich, John, and Ralph W. Duckwall. *Play Direction*. Englewood Cliffs, NJ: Prentice-Hall, 1983.

163

"Directing Issue," *Drama Review* (T54), June 1962.

Donkin, Ellen, and Susan Clement, eds. *Upstaging Big Daddy: Directing Theatre as if Race and Gender Matter.* Ann Arbor: University of Michigan Press, 1993.

Engel, Lehman. *Getting the Show On: The Complete Guidebook for Producing a Musical in Your Theatre.* New York: Schirmer, 1983.

Feral, Josette. "Mnouchkine's Workshop at the Soleil." *Drama Review* 33 (Winter, 1989).

Foreman, Richard. *Unbalancing Acts.* Ken Jordan, ed. New York: Pantheon Books, 1992.

Hodge, Francis. *Play Directing: Analysis, Communication and Style.* Rev. ed. Englewood Cliffs, NJ: Prentice-Hall, 1982.

Houseman, John. *Front and Center.* New York: Simon and Schuster, 1979.

Jones, David Richard. *Great Directors at Work: Stanislavsky, Brecht, Kazan, Brook.* Berkeley: University of California Press, 1986.

Kazan, Elia. "Excerpts from the Notebook Made in Preparation for Directing Arthur Miller's *Death of a Salesman* and Annotated Playscript." In Kenneth Thorpe Rowe, *A Theatre in Your Head.* New York: Funk and Wagnalls, 1960, pp. 44–59.

Kirk, John W., and Ralph A. Bellas. *The Art of Directing.* Belmont, CA: Wadsworth, 1985.

Lewis, Robert. *Method or Madness.* New York: Samuel French, 1958.

MacDonald, Heather. "On Peter Sellars." *Partisan Review* 58 (Fall 1991).

Marowitz, Charles. *Prospero's Staff: Acting and Directing in the Contemporary Theatre.* Bloomington: Indiana University Press, 1986.

McMullan, Frank. *The Directorial Image.* Hamden, CT: Shoe String, 1962.

Meyerhold, Vsevelod. *Meyerhold on Theatre.* Edward Braun, trans and ed. New York: Hill and Wang, 1969.

Miles-Brown, John. *Directing Drama.* London: Peter Owen, 1980.

Miller, Jonathan. *Subsequent Performances.* New York: Viking, 1986.

O'Neill, R. H., and N. M. Boretz. *The Director as Artist: Play Direction Today.* New York: Holt, Rinehart and Winston, 1987.

Roose-Evans, James. *Directing a Play.* New York: Theatre Arts, 1968.

Schneider, Alan. *Entrances.* New York: Viking Penguin, 1986.

Sellars, Peter. "Exits and Entrances: Peter Sellars on Opera." *Artforum* 28 (December 1989).

Shaw, Bernard. *The Art of Rehearsal.* New York: Samuel French, 1928.

Spolin, Viola. *Theatre Games for Rehearsal: A Director's Handbook.* Evanston, IL: Northwestern University Press, 1985.

Staub, August. *Creating Theatre: The Art of Theatrical Directing.* New York: Harper and Row, 1973.

Strasberg, Lee. *The Theatre Handbook.* Bernard Sobel, ed. New York: Crown, 1948, pp. 219–220.

Tairov, Alexander. *Notes of a Director.* William Kuhlke, trans. Coral Gables, FL: University of Miami Press, 1969.

Wills, J. Robert. *The Director in a Changing Theater: Essays on Theory and Practice.* Palo Alto, CA: Mayfield, 1976.

Acting

Allain, Paul. *The Art of Stillness: The Theater Practice of Tadashi Suzuki.* New York: Palgrave Macmillan, 2003.

Barker, Clive. *Theatre Games.* New York: Drama Books, 1977.

Benedetti, Robert L. *The Actor at Work.* 4th ed. Englewood Cliffs, NJ: Prentice-Hall, 1985.

———. *Seeming, Being and Becoming: Acting in Our Century.* New York: Drama Books, 1976.

Berry, Cicely. *Voice and the Actor.* London: Harrap, 1973.

Boal, Augusto. *Games for Actors and Non-Actors.* Adrian Jackson, trans. London and New York: Routledge, 1992.

Bogart, Anne. *A Director Prepares: Seven Essays on Art and Theatre.* New York: Routledge, 2001.

Boleslavski, Richard. *Acting: The First Six Lessons.* New York: Theatre Arts, 1963.

Callow, Simon. *Being an Actor.* New York: St. Martin's, 1984.

Cassady, Marsh. *Acting Games: Improvisations and Exercises.* Colorado Springs: Meriwether, 1993.

Chaikin, Joseph. *The Presence of the Actor.* New York: Macmillan, 1973.

Chekhov, Michael. *Lessons for the Professional Actor.* New York: Performing Arts Journal, 1985.

———. *To the Actor on the Technique of Acting.* New York: Harper and Brothers, 1953.

Cohen, Robert. *Acting Power: An Introduction to Acting.* Palo Alto, CA: Mayfield, 1978.

———. *Acting Professionally.* Palo Alto, CA: Mayfield, 1981.

Cole, David. *Acting as Reading: The Place of the Reading Process in the Actor's Work.* Ann Arbor: University of Michigan Press, 1992.

Cole, Toby. *Acting: A Handbook of the Stanislavsky Method.* New York: Crown, 1947.

Cole, Toby, and Helen Krich Chinoy. *Actors on Acting.* New York: Crown, 1980.

Crawford, Jerry, and Joan Snyder. *Acting in Person and in Style.* Dubuque, IA: W. C. Brown, 1976.

Delgado, Ramon. *Acting with Both Sides of Your Brain.* New York: Holt, Rinehart and Winston, 1986.

Funke, Lewis, and John E. Booth. *Actors Talking about Acting: Fourteen Interviews with Stars of the Theatre.* New York: Avon, 1973.

Grotowski, Jerzy. *Towards a Poor Theatre.* New York: Simon and Schuster, 1968.

Guthrie, Tyrone. *Tyron Guthrie on Acting.* New York: Viking, 1971.

Hagen, Uta, and Frankel Haskel. *Respect for Acting.* New York: Macmillan, 1973.

Harrop, John, and Sabin R. Epstein. *Acting with Style.* Englewood Cliffs, NJ: Prentice-Hall, 1982.

Huston, Hollis. *The Actor's Instrument.* Ann Arbor: University of Michigan Press, 1992.

Johnstone, Keith. *Impro: Improvisation and the Theatre.* London: Methuen, 1981.

Krasner, David. *Method Acting Reconsidered: Theory, Practice, Future.* New York: Palgrave Macmillan, 2000.

Laban, Rudolf. *The Mastery of Movement.* London: MacDonald and Evans, 1960.

Lessac, Arthur. *Body Wisdom: The Use and Training of the Human Body.* White Plains, NY: Lessac Research, 1978.

———. *The Use and Training of the Human Voice: A Practical Approach to Speech and Vocal Dynamics.* New York: DBS, 1967.

Lewis, Robert. *Method or Madness.* New York: Samuel French, 1958.

Linklatter, Kristen. *Freeing the Natural Voice.* New York: Drama Books, 1976.

McGaw, Charles. *Acting Is Believing.* 4th ed. New York: Holt, Rinehart and Winston, 1980.

Mekler, Eva. *New Generation of Acting Teachers.* New York: Penguin, 1987.

Olivier, Laurence. *On Acting.* New York: Simon and Schuster, 1986.

Penrod, James. *Movement for the Performing Artist.* Palo Alto, CA: National Press, 1974.

Redgrave, Michael. *The Actor's Ways and Means.* London: William Heinemann, 1953.

Russel, Douglas A. *Period Style for the Theatre.* Boston: Allyn and Bacon, 1980.

Saint-Denis, Michel. *Theatre: The Re-Discovery of Style.* New York: Theatre Arts, 1969.

———. *Training for the Theatre: Premises and Promises.* New York: Theatre Arts, 1982.

Shurtleff, Michael. *Audition.* New York: Walker, 1980.

Spolin, Viola. *Improvisation for the Theatre: A Handbook of Teaching and Directing Techniques.* Evanston, IL: Northwestern University Press, 1963.

Stanislavsky, Konstantin. *An Actor Prepares.* Elizabeth Reynolds Hapgood, ed. New York: Theatre Arts, 1937.

———. *An Actor's Handbook.* Elizabeth Reynolds Hapgood, ed. New York: Theatre Arts, 1963.

———. *Building a Character.* Elizabeth Reynolds Hapgood, ed. New York: Theatre Arts, 1968.

———. *Creating a Role.* Elizabeth Reynolds Hapgood, ed. New York: Theatre Arts, 1961.

Strasberg, Lee. *Strasberg at the Actors Studio.* Robert Hethmon, ed. New York: Viking Press, 1965.

Suzuki, Tadashi. *Way of Acting the Theatre: Writings of Tadashi Suzuki.* New York: Theatre Communications Group, 1986.

Design

Arnink, Donna J. *Creative Theatrical Makeup.* Englewood Cliffs, NJ: Prentice-Hall, 1984.

Aronson, Arnold. *American Theatre* 4 (October 24, 1987).

Appia, Adolph. *The Work of Living Art.* H. D. Albright, trans. Coral Gables, FL: University of Miami Press, 1960.

Bablet, Denis. *The Revolution of Stage Design in the Twentieth Century.* New York: Leon Amiel, 1977.

Barton, Lucy. *Historic Costume for the Stage.* Boston: Walter H. Baker, 1938.

———. *Appreciating Costume.* Boston: Walter H. Baker, 1969.

Bay, Howard. *Stage Design.* New York: Drama Books, 1978.

Boyle, Walden P., and John H. Jones. *Central and Flexible Staging.* Berkeley: University of California Press, 1956.

Buchman, Herman. *Stage Make-Up.* New York: Watson-Guptill, 1971.

Burdick, Elizabeth B., Peggy C. Hansen, Brenda Zanger. *Contemporary Stage Design USA.* Middletown, CT: Wesleyan University Press, 1975.

Burian, Jarka. *The Scenography of Josef Svoboda.* Middletown, CT: Wesleyan University Press, 1971.

Burris-Meyer, Harold, and Edward Cole. *Scenery for the Theatre.* 3rd ed. Boston: Little, Brown, 1972.

———. *Theatres and Auditoriums.* 2nd ed. New York: Van Nostrand Reinhold, 1964.

Calhoun, John. "Creating an Audio Environment." *Theatre Crafts* 23 (January 1989): 46–51.

Collison, David. *Stage Sound.* New York: Drama Books, 1976.

Corson, Richard. *Stage Makeup.* 6th ed. Englewood Cliffs, NJ: Prentice-Hall, 1981.

Craig, Edward Gordon. *On the Art of the Theatre.* New York: Theatre Arts, 1957.

———. *Scene.* London: H. Milford, 1923.

———. *The Theatre—Advancing.* Boston: Little, Brown, 1919.

———. *Towards a New Theatre: Forty Designs with Critical Notes.* London: J. M. Dent and Sons, 1913.

Davenport, Milia. *Book of Costume,* 2 vols. New York: Crown, 1948.

Dolman, John, Jr., and Richard K. Knaub. *The Art of Play Production.* 3rd ed. New York: Harper and Row, 1973.

Essig, Linda. *Lighting and the Design Idea.* Belmont, CA: International Thomson, 1996.

———. *The Speed of Light: Dialogues on Lighting Design and Technological Change.* London: Heinemann, 2002.

Fischer, Howard T. "An Introduction to Color." In James M. Carpenter, ed., *Color in Art.* Cambridge, MA: Fogg Art Museum, 1974.

Gassner, John. *Form and Idea in Modern Theatre.* New York: Dryden, 1956.

Gillette, Arnold S. *An Introduction to Scene Design.* New York: Harper and Row, 1967.

Glass, Philip. *Music by Philip Glass.* New York: Harper and Row, 1987.

Heffner, Huburt C., Samuel Selden, and Hunton D. Sellman. *Modern Theatre Practice: A Handbook of Play Production.* 4th ed. New York: Appleton-Century-Crofts, 1959.

Itten, Johannes. *The Art of Color.* New York: Reinhold, 1961.

Jones, Robert Edmund. *The Dramatic Imagination.* New York: Theatre Arts, 1941.

Kaye, Deena, and James LeBrecht. *Sound and Music for the Theatre.* New York: Backstage Books, 1992.

———. *Sound and Music for the Theatre: The Art and Technique of Design.* 2nd ed. Burlington, MA: Focal, 1999.

Kueppers, Harald. *The Basic Law of Color Theory.* Roger Marcinik, trans. Woodbury, NY: Barron's, 1982.

McKim, Robert H. *Thinking Visually.* Belmont, CA: Wadsworth, 1980.

Mielziner, Jo. *Designing for the Theatre.* New York: Atheneum, 1965.

———. *The Shapes of Our Theatre.* C. Ray Smith, ed. New York: Charles N. Potter, 1970.

Motley, Pseud. *Theatre Props.* New York: Drama Publishers, 1977.

Papanek, Victor. *Design for the Real World: Human Ecology and Social Change.* New York: Pantheon, 1967.

Pecktal, Lyn. *Costume Design: Techniques of Modern Masters.* New York: Watson-Guptill, 1999.

———. *Designing and Drawing for the Theater.* New York: McGraw-Hill, 1994.

———. *Designing and Painting for the Theatre.* New York: Holt, Rinehart and Winston, 1975.

Rosenthal, Jean, and Lael Wertenbaker. *The Magic of Light.* Boston: Little, Brown, 1972.

Russell, Douglas A. *Period Style for the Theatre.* Boston: Allyn and Bacon, 1980.

———. *Stage Costume Design.* Englewood Cliffs, NJ: Prentice-Hall, 1973.

———. *Theatrical Style: A Visual Approach to Theatre.* Palo Alto, CA: Mayfield, 1976.

Simonsen, Lee. *The Art of Scenic Design.* New York: Greenwood, 1973.

———. *The Stage Is Set.* New York: Theatre Arts, 1963.

Playwriting

Bentley, Eric. *The Playwright at Thinker.* New York: Atheneum, 1967.

Brecht, Bertolt. *Playwrights on Playwriting.* Toby Cole, ed. New York: Hill and Wang, 1960.

Catron, Louis E. *Writing, Producing, and Selling Your Play.* Englewood Cliffs, NJ: Prentice-Hall, 1984.

Chekhov, Michael. *To the Director and Playwright.* Charles Leonard, ed. and comp. New York: Harper and Row, 1963.

Hornby, Richard. *Script into Performance.* New York: Paragon, 1987.

Kerr, Walter. *How Not to Write a Play.* New York: Simon and Schuster, 1955.

Savran, David, ed. *In Their Own Words: Contemporary American Playwrights.* New York: Theatre Communications Group, 1988.

———. *The Wooster Group, 1975–1985: Breaking the Rules.* Ann Arbor: UMI Research Press, 1986.

Theatre Communications Group. *Dramatists Sourcebook, 2002–3 Edition: Complete Opportunities for Playwrights, Translators, Composers, Lyricists and Librettists.* New York: Theatre Communications Group, 2002.

Dramaturgy

Bly, Mark, Shelby Jiggets, Jim Lewis, Paul Walsh, and Christopher Baker. *The Production Notebooks: Theatre in Process.* New York: Theatre Communications Group, 1996.

Cardullo, Bert. *What Is Dramaturgy?* New York: Peter Lang Publishing, 2000.

Ensembles

Beck, Julian. *The Life of the Theatre.* San Francisco: City Lights, 1972.

———. *Paradise Now,* "A Collective Creation of The Living Theatre Written Down by Judith Malina and Julian Beck." New York: Random House, 1971.

Brecht, Bertolt. *Brecht on Theatre: The Development of an Aesthetic.* John Willet, ed. and trans. New York: Hill and Wang, 1964.

Clurman, Harold. *The Fervent Years: The Story of the Group Theater and the Thirties.* New York: Harcourt, 1975.

Mantegna, Granfranco, and Aldo Rostagno, with Julian Beck and Judith Malina. *We, The Living Theatre.* New York: Ballantine, 1970.

Theater History and Theory

Arnheim, Rudolph. *Art and Visual Perception: A Psychology of the Creative Eye.* Los Angeles: University of California Press, 1974.

Artaud, Antonin. *The Theatre and Its Double.* Mary Caroline Richard, trans. New York: Grove, 1958.

Bablet, Dennis. *Edward Gordon Craig.* Daphne Woodward, trans. New York: Theatre Arts, 1966.

Barba, Eugenio, and Ludwik Flaszen. *A Dictionary of Theatre Anthropology.* Richard Fowler, trans. London: Routledge, 1991.

Barranger, Milly S. *Theatre: A Way of Seeing.* Belmont, CA: Wadsworth, 1986.

Barthes, Roland. *Elements of Seminology.* Annette Lavers and Colin Smith, trans. New York: Hill and Wang, 1967.

Bennet, Susan. *Theatre Audiences.* New York: Routledge, 1990.

Bentley, Eric. *In Search of Theatre.* New York: Alfred A. Knopf, 1953.

Bergson, Henri. "Laughter." In Wylie Sypher, ed., *Comedy.* Garden City, NY: Doubleday, 1956.

Biner, Pierre. *The Living Theatre.* Far Hill, NJ: Horizon, 1972.

Blau, Herbert. *The Impossible Theatre.* New York: Macmillan, 1964.

Braun, Edward. *The Director and the Stage: From Naturalism to Grotowski.* New York: Holmes and Meier, 1982.

Brockett, Oscar G. *History of the Theatre.* 5th ed. Boston: Allyn and Bacon, 1987.

Brook, Peter. *The Empty Space.* New York: Atheneum, 1968.

———. *The Shifting Point: Theatre, Film, Opera, 1946–1987.* New York: Harper and Row, 1987.

Brustein, Robert. *Reimagining American Theatre.* New York: Hill and Wang, 1991.

———. *Revolution as Theatre: Notes on the New Radical Style.* New York: W.W. Norton, 1970.

———. *Seasons of Discontent: Dramatic Opinions, 1959–1965.* New York: Simon and Schuster, 1965.

———. *The Theatre of Revolt.* Boston: Little, Brown, 1964.

Cage, John. *Silence: Lectures and Writings.* Middletown, CT: Wesleyan University Press, 1961.

Carlson, Marvin. *Places of Performance: The Semiotics of Theatre Architecture.* Ithaca, NY: Cornell University Press, 1989.

———. *Theatre Semiotics.* Bloomington: Indiana University Press, 1990.

Case, Sue-Ellen. *Feminism and Theatre.* London: Methuen, 1988.

Cirlot, J. E. *A Dictionary of Symbols.* New York: Philosophical Library, 1962.

Contemporary Arts Center, Cincinnati, and Byrd Hoffman Foundation. *The Theatre of Images.* Rev. ed. New York: Harper and Row, 1984.

Copeland, Roger. "Master of the Body." *American Theatre* 1 (May 1988): 14–15.

Corrigan, Robert W. *Comedy: Meaning and Form.* San Francisco: Chandler, 1965.

———. *Tragedy: Vision and Form.* San Francisco: Chandler, 1965.

Davy, Kate. *Richard Foreman and the Ontological-Hysteric Theatre.* Ann Arbor: UMI Research Press, 1981.

Dolan, Jill. *The Feminist Spectator as Critic.* Ann Arbor: UMI Research Press, 1988.

Durham, Weldon B. *American Theatre Companies, 1931–1986.* New York: Greenwood, 1989.

Eco, Umberto. *A Theory of Semiotics.* Bloomington: Indiana University Press, 1976.

Elam, Keir. *The Semiotics of Theatre and Drama.* New York: Routledge, 2002.

Esslin, Martin. *Brecht: The Man and His Works.* Garden City, NY: Doubleday, 1971.

———. *Theatre of the Absurd.* Garden City, NY: Doubleday, 1969.

Freytag, Gustav. *Technique of the Drama.* Chicago: Griggs, 1895.

Frye, Northrop. *Anatomy of Criticism: Four Essays.* Princeton, NJ: Princeton University Press, 1974.

George, Kathleen. *Rhythm in Drama.* Pittsburgh: University of Pittsburgh Press, 1980.

Gorchakov, Nikolai M. *Stanislavsky Directs.* Miriam Goldina, trans. New York: Funk and Wagnalls, 1954.

———. *The Vakhtangov School of Stage Art.* Moscow: Foreign Languages, 1950.

Gropius, Walter, ed. *The Theatre of the Bauhaus.* Middletown, CT: Wesleyan University Press, 1971.

Grube, Max. *The Story of the Meininger.* Wendell Cole., ed., Anne Marie Koller, trans. Coral Gables, FL: University of Miami Press, 1963.

Hansen, Al. *A Primer of Happenings and Time/Space Art.* New York: Something Else, 1965.

Hayman, Ronald. *Theatre and Anti-Theatre: New Movements since Beckett.* New York: Oxford University Press, 1979.

Kaprow, Allan. *Assemblages, Environments and Happenings.* New York: H. N. Abrams, 1966.

Kirby, E. T., ed. *Total Theatre: A Critical Anthology.* New York: E. P. Dutton, 1969.

Kott, Jan. "After Grotowski." *Theatre Quarterly* 10 (Summer 1980): 27–32.

Langer, Suzanne K. *Feeling and Form.* New York: Charles Scribner's Sons, 1953.

Ley, Maria Piscator. *The Piscator Experiment: The Political Theatre.* Carbondale: Southern Illinois University Press, 1970.

Nagler, A. M. *Sources of Theatrical History.* New York: Theatre Annual, 1952.

Nemirovitch-Dantchenko, Vladimir. *My Life in Russian Theatre.* John Cournos, trans. New York: Theatre Arts, 1987.

Nicoll, Allardyce. *The Development of the Theatre.* New York: Harcourt Brace Jovanovich, 1958.

Pavis, Patrice. *Languages of the Stage.* New York: Performing Arts Journal, 1982.

Schechner, Richard. *Environmental Theatre.* New York: Hawthorne, 1973.

Shyer, Laurence. *Robert Wilson and His Collaborators.* New York: Theatre Communications Group, 1989.

Stanislavsky, Konstantin. *My Life in Art.* New York: Theatre Arts, 1948.

———. *Stanislavsky on the Art of the Stage.* David Magarshack, trans. London: Faber and Faber, 1950.

Stebbings, Genevieve. *Delsarte System of Expression.* Belmar, NJ: Edgar S. Werner, 1902.

Steele, Mike. "The Romanian Directors." *American Theatre* 2 (July–August 1985): 4–11.

Sterritt, David. "With Ibsen Play, Wilson Opens New Chapter in His 'Theatre of Images.'" *Christian Science Monitor* 21 (February 1991).

Styan, J. L. *Drama, Stage and Audience.* London: Cambridge University Press, 1975.

Toporkov, Vasily Osipovich. *Stanislavsky in Rehearsal: The Final Years.* Christine Edwards, trans. New York: Theatre Arts, 1979.

Turner, Victor. *The Anthropology of Performance.* New York: Performing Arts Journal, 1986.

Willet, John. *The Theatre of Bertolt Brecht.* New York: New Directions, 1959.

Williams, David. *Peter Brook: A Theoretical Casebook.* London: Methuen, 1988.

Wills, J. Robert, ed. *The Director in a Changing Theatre.* Palo Alto, CA: Mayfield, 1976.

Management

Farber, Donald C. *From Option to Opening.* 3rd ed. New York: Drama Books, 1977.
———. *Producing on Broadway.* New York: Drama Books, 1969.
Langley, Stephen. *Producers on Producing.* New York: Drama Books, 1976.
———. *Theatre Management in America.* New York: Drama Books, 1974.
Newman, Danny. *Subscribe Now! Building Arts Audience through Dynamic Subscription Promotion.* New York: Drama Books, 1977.
Reiss, Alvin H., ed. *Market the Arts!* New York: FEDAPT, 1983.
———. *The Arts Management Handbook.* New York: Law-Arts, 1970.

Publicity

Ashford, Gerald. *Everyday Publicity: A Practical Guide.* New York: Law-Arts, 1970.
Capbern, A. Martial. *The Drama Publicist.* New York: Pageant, 1968.
Levine, Mindy N., and Susan Frank. *In Print.* Englewood Cliffs, NJ: Prentice-Hall, 1984.
Melcher, Daniel, and Nancy Larrick. *Printing and Promotion.* New York: McGraw-Hill, 1956.
Skal, David J. *Graphic Communications for the Performing Arts.* New York: Theatre Communications Group, 1981.

INDEX

A

acting, suggested readings for, 165–66
action, 51
  analysis, 27–32
  defined, 56–57
  and objectives, 55–59 (*See also* textual
    elements)
Akalaitis, Joanne, 93
Albee, Edward, 37
Allen, Woody, 16
analysis
  action, 27–32
  character, 44
  script, 35, 98–99
  summary of character traits for, 71
Annie Hall, 16
Antoine, André, 93
approval, 92
asymmetrical compositions, 83, 86
audition, 135–39
  form, 144
  goals, 138–39
Audition (Shurtleff), 56, 59

B

And Baby Makes Seven, 37
Backwards and Forwards (Ball), 29
Baitz, Jon Robin, 37
balanced compositions, 86
balancing
  idealism and pragmatism, 18
  leadership and collaboration, 16–20
Ball, David, 29
Ball, William, 57
The Baltimore Waltz, 109–10
  design process, 109–10
Beckett, Samuel, 93
Betrayal, 36, 89, 105
The Birthday Party, 111–12
  design process, 112
Blue Window, 37
Body Beautiful, 78
Boy Gets Girl, 37
brainstorming phase, 118
Brecht, Bertolt, 52
Burn This, 37
business, 88

C

callbacks, 138
Carra, Lawrence, 82
casting, 135–39
  one-act plays, 137–38

Caucasian Chalk Circle, 52
causality, 51
centrality, 28
character, 68–71
  analysis, 44
  traits for analysis, summary of, 71
character(s), 29–30, 51
  number of, 30–31
  relationships and status, 71–75
checklist
  dramaturgy, 99–100
  producing, 148
  script analysis, 98–99
Chekhov, Anton, 93
The Cherry Orchard, 93
choreographers, 132
Chronegk, Ludwig, 3
climactic plays, 51
climactic structure, 51–54. *See also* textual
  elements
Clurman, Harold, 6
Cohen, Robert, 15
collaboration
  defining, 2–5
  design, 101–27
  and leadership, 15–20
  in rehearsal, 35–46
  responsibilities of, 8–9
  terms that emphasize, 17–18
composing in found environments, 83, 85
composition, 82
concept, 6
confidence, 19–20
conflict, 19
core action, 6–8, 21–33, 44, 98
  action analysis, 27–32
  statements, 104–6
  story and plot, 21–27
costume
  designer, 121
  parade, 123
counter, 82
countering, 86
course outline form, 151
Creative Play Direction (Cohen and
  Harrop), 15
cue-to-cue, 122

D

Dean, Alexander, 82
dependability, 19–20
design, suggested readings for, 166–67

173

design collaboration, 101–27
  core action statements, 104–6
design process
  The Baltimore Waltz, 109–10
  The Birthday Party, 112
  Hedda Gabler, 107
  Twelfth Night, 114
design timetable, 117–24
  brainstorming phase, 118
  implementation phase, 121
  initial design meeting, 117–18
  rendering and model phase, 118–21
  technical/dress rehearsals, 121–24
directing, suggested reading for, 163–64
directing elements, 47–100
  integrating, 96–98
  textual, 49–76
  visceral, 76–95
A Doll House, 93
Don Giovanni, 93
Dr. Strangelove, 109
dramaturgs, 131–32
  protocol, 131
  tasks of, 132
dramaturgy
  checklist, 99–100
  suggested reading for, 168
dress rehearsals, 121–24
dry tech, 122
dynamic compositions, 86

E
Eastern Standard, 37
Endgame, 93
ensemble, 9
  created sound, 81
  energizing the, 17–18
  suggested readings for, 168
environment, 31–32, 92–94. *See also* visceral elements
  exercises, 94
environmental sound, 80
epic, 52
episodic plays, 51–52
episodic structure, 51–54. *See also* textual elements
events, 28–29
exercises
  action and objective, 58–59
  character choices, 69
  compositions, 83
  core action, 25
  environment, 94
  gesture, 91
  groundplan, 62, 64–65
  language, 75–76
  movement, 90

relationship and status, 72–74
  shifts in scene, 60–61
  sound, 80–81
  structure, 50, 52
  style, 95
  tempo, 79
  time, 54–55

F
fine tuning, 44
first read-through, 44
first scene collaboration, 38–42
Fool for Love, 37
forms
  audition, 144
  course outline, 151
  poster information, 150
  producing checklist, 148
  program information, 149
  project proposal, 142
  rehearsal observation, 147
  sample audition notice, 143
  sample callback, 145
  sample cast list, 146
found space, 87
frames, 82
framing and filling, 83
full-color model, 121
Fundamentals of Play Directing (Dean and Carra), 82
fundamental techniques, 9–13

G
genre improvisation, 95
gesture, 91–92. *See also* visceral elements
  exercises, 91
  personal, 92
Gilman, Rebecca, 37
goals, defining and reaching, 19
Greenberg, Richard, 37
Grotowski, Jerzy, 38
groundplan, 62–68, 82. *See also* textual elements
  exercises, 62
Group Theater, 6
Gutierrez, Gerry, 4

H
Hamlet, 30
Harrop, John, 15
Hawking, Judith, 4
Hedda Gabler, 52, 93
  design process, 107
  sample scene breakdown for, 53
How I Learned to Drive, 37

I
Ibsen, Henrik, 18, 52, 93, 106 7
idealism and pragmatism, balancing, 18
Iizuka, Naomi, 68, 78
implementation phase, 121
impressions, 91–92
Impro (Johnstone), 69
in-class observations, 44
indifference, 92
initial design meeting, 117–18
inspiration, 27
instructor observations, 44
integrating directing elements, 96–98
Ivanov, 4

J
Johnstone, Keith, 69

K
keeping order, 19
key moment, 59–61
King Lear, 30, 83
Klavan, Laurence, 22–25
Kline, Kevin, 4

L
language, 75–76. *See also* textual elements
leadership
   and collaboration, 15–20
   terms that emphasize, 18–19
Lepage, Robert, 36
Life Under Water, 37
lighting looks, 120
light plot, 120
listening to others, 18
literary manager, 131, 134
Living Theater, 3
Lobby Hero, 37
Lonnergan, Kenneth, 37
Lucas, Craig, 37

M
Mabou Mines, 3
Macbeth, 120
making choices, 18–19
Mamet, David, 75
management, suggested reading for, 171
Ma Rainey's Black Bottom, 37
Matthews, Nathan, 133
McDonald, Linda, 89
mediating conflict, 19
Meiningen Players, 3
Miller, Arthur, 37, 48
Miss Julie, 93
mock audition, 137
mood, 79–81

Mother Courage and Her Children, 52
movement, 87 91. *See also* visceral elements
   exercises, 90
music directors, 132, 133

N
The New Rules, 22–27, 30, 31
   playwright's intentions, 26
   sample unit score from, 96–98
Norgren, Catherine, 104

O
objective, 55–59, 57
observations
   in-class, 44
   instructor, 44
   peer, 44–45
   rehearsal, 44–46
   rules for, 45–46
off-book, 44
Old Times, 13, 36–37
The Old Woman Broods, 87
one-act plays, casting, 137–38
O'Neill National Theatre Institute, 2
overall action-objectives, 44
overall arc, 44

P
pace, 77
paper tech, 121
peer observations, 44–45
personal
   gestures, 92
   point of view, 45
photo call, 123
The Piano Lesson, 37
picturization, 82, 86
Pinter, Harold, 13, 36, 111–12
places, 51
playwrights, 129–30
   readings and staged readings, 129–30
playwriting, suggested readings for, 168
plot
   defined, 21
   sound, 81
   story and, 21–27
ploy, 51
Poetics, 21
point of attack, 51
poor theater, 38
poster information form, 150
preparation, 42–44
private space, 90
problem solving, 11–12
producing checklist, 148

production dramaturgs, 131, 134
program information, 149
project proposal form, 142
psychological gesture, 92
publicity, suggested reading for, 171
public space, 90

R
reading, 129, 133
receiver, 57
Reckless, 37
redirecting focus, 19
Redwood Curtain, 37
rehearsal, 35–46
    first scene collaboration, 38–42
    observations, 37, 44–46
    preparation, 42–44
    sample schedule, 44
    units, 44
    videotaping, 46
rejection, 92
relationship
    characters, 71–75
    exercise, 72, 74
rendering and model phase, 118–21
research support, 28
respecting others, 18
responsibilities, collaboration, 8–9
rhythm, 77–79. *See also* visceral elements
    defined, 79
The Ride Down Mt. Morgan, 37
role-playing exercises, 10
Rózewicz, Tadeusz, 87
run-throughs, 44

S
sample
    audition notice, 143
    callback, 145
    cast list, 146
    rehearsal schedule, 44
scale models, 120
scenes, 51
script analysis, 35
    checklist for, 98–99
script analysis, elements of, 28–32
    character, 29–30
    environment and number of settings,
        31–32
    events, 28–29
    number of characters, 30–31
    sound, 32
Sellars, Peter, 93
A Sense of Direction (Ball), 57
set designers, 118, 120
settings, number of, 31–32

Shakespeare, William, 113–17
Shaw, George Bernard, 49
Shephard, Sam, 37
shifts, 59–61
Shurtleff, Michael, 56, 59
simulation exercises, 10
social circles, 92
societal gesture, 92
sound, 32, 79–81
    environmental, 80
    exercises, 80–81
    plot, 81
    selecting, 80
    stylized, 81
space, 91
specificity, 27
spine, 6
Spinning into Butter, 37
staged reading, 129, 133
status, 71–75
    character, 71–72
    exercise, 74
story
    defined, 21
    and plot, 21–27
Strindberg, August, 93
structure, 49–51, 98. *See also* textual ele-
    ments
    climactic and episodic, 51–54
    exercises, 52
style, 94–95. *See also* visceral elements
    exercises, 95
stylized sound, 81
Substance of Fire, 37
super-objective, 56
swatches, 121
symmetrical compositions, 83, 86

T
table scene exercise, 90
tag audition, 138
Tattoo Girl, 68
team writing, 10
technical rehearsals, 121–24
techniques, fundamental, 9–13
tempo, 77–79. *See also* visceral elements
    defined, 79
    exercises, 79
territory exercise, 90
textual elements, 49–76. *See also* directing
    elements
    actions and objectives, 55–59
    character, 68–71
    climactic and episodic structure, 51–54
    groundplan, 62–68
    language, 75–76

relationships and status, 71–75
shifts and key moments, 59–61
structure, 49–51
textual evidence, 28
The Theater Experience, 51
theater history and theory, suggested
    reading for, 168–70
The Third Man, 109
This Is My Youth, 37
The Three Sisters, 93
Three Tall Women, 37
thumbnail sketches, 118
time exercises, 54–55
timetable, design, 117–24
touch-up, 44
Towards a Poor Theatre, 38
transitions, 81
True West, 37
Twelfth Night, 30, 113–17
    design process, 114

U
Uncle Vanya, 93
underscoring, 80
unit breakdown, 98
unit titles, 98

V
videotaping rehearsals, 46
A View from the Bridge, 37
visceral elements, 76–95. *See also* directing
    elements
    environment, 92–94
    gesture, 91–92
    movement, 87–91
    sound and mood, 79–81
    style, 94–95
    tempo and rhythm, 77–79
    visual composition, 82–87
Vogel, Paula, 37, 109–10

W
Waco Woman, 89
white models, 120
Williams, Tennessee, 48
Wilson, Edwin, 51
Wilson, Lanford, 37
workshop productions, 130, 133
writing-to-learn exercises, 10

Z
Zola, Emile, 93
The Zoo Story, 37